THE ASH GROVE

ii

THIS TYPICAL WARWICKSHIRE SCENE OF HAYMAKING IN THE EARLY 1930s SHOWS TED MASTERS AND FRANK ROBERTS ON THE MOWER. The house still stands but the field is now occupied by the houses and shops of Home Farm Crescent and the beautiful elms are gone. (MM)

THE ASH GROVE
Jean Field

The History of Whitnash in Words and Pictures

SUNKEN BELL PRODUCTIONS

This book is dedicated
to
my brother Ian A.H. Box

THE FRONT COVER shows a watercolour (believed to have been painted by Tom Baker in the late 1830s) in which the rear of Green Farm, as seen from the Whitnash Road near the Doglands, is clearly recognisable. This painting is now in a private collection in Worcestershire.

First published in 1996 by SUNKEN BELL PRODUCTIONS, 11 Watersfield Gardens, Leamington Spa, Warwickshire CV31 1NT

ISBN   0 9528191 0 4

Printed in England by SALVO PRINT, Royal Leamington Spa.

CONTENTS

FOREWORD

A MESSAGE FROM THE CHAIRMAN OF
THE WHITNASH SOCIETY

It is my privilege to be Chairman of the Whitnash Society coincident with the publication of this latest book by Jean Field. As with her previous books, Jean has provided a great sense of interest, history and humour concerning the development of Whitnash from its status as a village to that of a small town.

I feel sure that the book will be a great success and that it will provide useful information for many present and future readers, desirous to know more about this interesting Warwickshire town.

Stanley Warmington
Whitnash
March 1996

INTRODUCTION

On 15th May 1993 "Beneath the Great Elms" my previous book on Whitnash was published. Around 100 people gathered in the Community Centre in Acre Close to watch Bernard Kirton, the First Mayor of Whitnash, being presented with a specially signed copy and local historian, Shirley Reading, making a short speech. Several people who had grown up in Whitnash in years past travelled many miles to be present for the occasion and Jean Pailing (née Addicott) Michael Jacobs, Valerie Jacobs (née Taylor), Margaret Lomas (née Gleave) and numerous others had a delightful reunion with family and friends still living in Warwickshire. Entertainment was provided by the long-established Whitnash Church Handbell Ringers and at my request amongst the tunes they played was "The Ash Grove" for I felt it appropriate.

There was such a favourable reaction to "Beneath the Great Elms" and so many ex-residents offered to lend old photographs or tell me their reminiscences that I determined there should be this second book to supplement the first and fill in many of the gaps. The title of this book was thus an obvious choice and in my first chapter readers will learn of the great significance of ash trees in general and the Whitnash Ash in particular.

Inevitably in "Beneath the Great Elms" there were a couple of mistakes concerning names, which were pointed out to me afterwards. In good faith I had taken names printed on the back of photographs to be those people portrayed there, but to any readers who felt aggrieved that I had not mentioned them by name under the photograph or worse still had referred to them as someone else, I wholeheartedly apologise! I had no means of knowing (until the book appeared) that the names supplied were incorrect and it is extremely difficult to check such things for people's memories are not always accurate.

It appeared that "Beneath the Great Elms" stirred many emotions and jogged at least one conscience for within a day of the book being reported in the local press, I received an anonymous telephone call from an elderly gentleman who confessed to damaging the clock on St Margaret's Church when a teenager in the 1930s! Within a few weeks of the launch I had been invited to take part in a live radio interview at the C.W.R. radio studio in West Orchard Shopping Centre in Coventry and a group of enthusiasts had decided to form the "Whitnash Society".

Sadly since 1993 a number of those connected with "Beneath the Great Elms" have died. Gerald Cox who loaned me many photographs, related many anecdotes and together with his wife Freda did so much to make the publicity launch such a success, died in June 1994. Also other friends such as Bill Bailey of Haseley Close, Bert Bean, Margaret Lomas (née Gleave) and others died within the past three years, but they are still fondly remembered by many in the area.

Although I have lived most of my life in or near Whitnash and am in touch with many of the older residents, it is difficult to know which photographs and items to include in a book. I find the entire history of Whitnash interesting and to be forced to reject half of the available material for reasons of space is very frustrating. I feel I must apologise to those who have lent me photographs which I have not been able to use here —— it may well be that in the future there is another book and already I have quite a lot of material saved up for that!

ON 15TH MAY 1993 "BENEATH THE GREAT ELMS" WAS LAUNCHED AND THE IDEA FOR THIS BOOK TOOK SHAPE! In this photograph I am presenting the Mayor of Whitnash Bernard Kirton with a specially signed copy and we are both wearing buttonholes kindly made and donated by Doreen Halford of Coppice Road to make the occasion more festive. Also seen are the long-established Whitnash Church Handbell Ringers who are (left to right) Ann Moffat, Linda Stevens, John Harris, Ray King , Jim Harris and Ian Stevens. (Photograph courtesy of Leamington Spa Courier)

GERALD COX, PICTURED HERE AT THE LAUNCH OF "BENEATH THE GREAT ELMS" DID MUCH TO MAKE THAT BOOK A SUCCESS. Not only did he loan many photographs from his vast collection of archives, but also, together with his wife Freda, he took charge of the refreshments at the launch. Gerald's death in June 1994 at the age of 65 robbed the town of Whitnash of one of its most enthusiastic citizens. (Photograph courtesy of Observer Newspapers)

4

EARLY HISTORY

EARLY HISTORY AND THE MEANING OF THE NAME OF WHITNASH

The earliest meaning (suggested by Sir William Dugdale in 1656) was *'THE PLACE NEAR THE WOOD'* from two Celtic words but the name *"WHITNASH"* is usually explained as meaning *'AT THE WHITE ASH'* translated from Anglo Saxon. Other interpretations include *'FAIR ASH'*, *'SPLENDID ASH'*, *'SACRED ASH'* or *'THE MEETING PLACE OF THE WISE MEN'*. If the first explanation of Celtic words were true, then perhaps the wood in question could have been Highdown Wood, supposed by many to be an ancient site, but maybe instead of wood, *TREE* or *TREES* could have been meant.

Whatever version is preferred, it would appear that nearly all of these explanations are linked for many ancient peoples revered ash trees. The fruits of the ash tree were considered a delicacy which possessed medicinal properties. Articles made from ash wood were frequently found in burial mounds and the numerous superstitions as to how ash trees could cure a variety of illnesses have been described by writers as diverse as Pliny, John Evelyn and Gilbert White.

It may have been that in prehistoric times Whitnash possessed a MARK TREE used for meetings, for the settlement is on at least one Ley line, as described by Alfred Watkins in "the Old Straight Track", first published in 1925. Watkins mentions Whitnash as having a name combining a tree and leyline and he said that one ley (or prehistoric track) went from Catesby through the mounds on which Southam and Whitnash Churches stand and on to the mound at Warwick Castle. It is generally accepted that parts of the Fosse Way (the road which forms the southern boundary of Whitnash) were in existence long before the Romans arrived and indeed pointers that a 3000 year old settlement existed close to the Fosse near Radford Semele were identified in 1973.

Ash trees grow well in meadows and valleys close to running water, and therefore sacred ash trees were very often found close to holy wells, which were also situated on leys. Celtic peoples revered trees, wells and springs in particular and as Whitnash possesses the site of an ancient holy well, the name of the settlement would seem appropriate.

Many superstitions concerning ash trees come from Scandinavian mythology which spoke of the ash as *YGGDRASIL* or *THE TREE OF LIFE* whose roots and branches connected earth, heaven and hell. At its root was a fountain of wonderful virtues.

The wood of the ash is firm, but pliable, and as such was used for making staves capable of withstanding a great strain. In "The Iliad" the Greek poet, Homer, described how the heroes carried spears made from ash wood.

A few years ago, in a talk on the radio, a historian (his name forgotten by those who heard the programme) suggested that in the legend where Morvidus, a ruler of Warwick in Celtic times slew a giant with a young ash tree which he tore up by its roots, the sapling originated in Whitnash, which was easily accessible from Warwick. This legend has given rise to the present "ragged staff" emblem, first adopted by the Earls of Warwick and later by the County itself.

Thus it can be seen that the very name of 'WHITNASH' apparently associated with one important ash tree has various historical implications. Both in Celtic and Saxon times, important tribal assemblies were frequently held alongside such sacred trees and groves.

The artificial mound on which Whitnash Church is situated was said to be a site of great pagan significance and around 1900 the respected historian Mr S.S. Stanley thought that this site in Whitnash had been an Ancient British encampment and that a skirmish with Romans from the camp at Chesterton had taken place there. He based his assumption on Roman fastenings and other items found near to the church. Several Roman coins have been unearthed in this area over a period of many years and a coin dating from the 3rd or 4th century was found fairly recently.

In his "History and Description of the Parish of Whitnash", published in 1865, Canon Young described how Roman coins of an early date had been dug up from the stonework of a house in Whitnash, close to the Roman camp at Chesterton. Also there have been other Roman coins found in the Heathcote Road area, in the 1950s.

Another pointer towards possible Celtic occupation was provided in 1976 when a Celtic coin dating from around 40 A.D. was found near the top of Ashford Road . The coin, which shows a horse and wheel, belonged to the Dobunni tribe which occupied

IN 1976 A GOLD COIN OF THE DOBUNNI TRIBE DATING FROM 40 A.D. WAS FOUND NEAR ASHFORD ROAD. The coin is only two centimetres in diameter and on one side is depicted a horse and a wheel and on the other is an ear of corn. Both the horse and wheel are traditional Celtic symbols, the horse sig-nifying speed, beauty, and sexual prowess and the wheel being a symbol of the sun and solar deities. (Photograph reproduced by permission of Warwickshire Museum)

Worcestershire, Gloucestershire and the southern part of Warwickshire at that period.
A large stone axe, possibly 3,000 years old, was also found in Whitnash around 50
years ago, but details of the find are unclear.

THE HOLY WELL

Celtic people revered natural phenomena such as wells, springs and trees and eight
river names in Warwickshire are said to be of Celtic origin including the Avon (meaning
'River') and the Leam (meaning 'Elms'). Near the Whitnash Brook, which flows into the

*THIS AERIAL PHOTOGRAPH (TAKEN BY TOM ROBERTS FOR THE WHITNASH SOCIETY
IN 1994) SHOWS THE WHITNASH BROOK VALLEY AND THE SITES OF HISTORICAL
IMPORTANCE.*

Leam, there was once a holy well and this was first described by Tom Burgess in his book "Historic Warwickshire" published in 1875. A respected Midlands journalist and Editor of the Leamington Spa Courier, Burgess took the trouble to seek out and record for posterity many old legends, visiting nearly every parish in Warwickshire before he wrote his book. His work is generally accepted as being reliable and this extract concerning Whitnash was quoted in an H.M.S.O. book "The Wells and Springs of Warwickshire" in 1928.

Burgess wrote, *"There was formerly an ancient well by the side of Whitnash brook, to the south of the footway from Whitnash to Radford, and concerning which this curious legend is told:- That the ancient inhabitants, when removing the bell from the ancient church to its present site, brought it to this holy well to be freshly consecrated. In doing this it fell into the water and gradually disappeared. The country people, who wish to know coming events, cast stones into the well at night, and in the morning their questions are answered by the sounding of the bell.*

The site is now drained, but the little stream of water which flows into the Whitnash brook is still believed to be possessed of healing power and people come from great distances to procure the water".

In recent years enthusiasts from The Whitnash Society have identified the site of the well and stream as described by Burgess. In 1994 a number of pieces of 19th century pottery were found at the site, this pottery probably being used as infill when the site was drained, perhaps around 1850 when the field enclosures took place.

A short time ago, in early 1996, Mr D. T. N. Booth of Halesowen (teacher, author and member of the Midland Wind and Watermills Group) visited the site along with myself and two others. Being experienced in the interpretation of sites connected with springs, wells and mills, Tim Booth expressed great interest and said that he was as sure as one could be without excavation, that the site identified was that as described by Burgess. An old drain (19th century?) provided most of the water flow for the tiny stream into the brook and the amount of water suggested that it came from a spring.

Holy wells were generally sited on leys and both the holy well at Whitnash and the existing holy well at Southam would be on or close to the ley from Catesby to Warwick. On the Radford bank, there appears to be some evidence of a former track leading to a crossing point over the brook, close to the well site and this track is directly in line with Whitnash Church which is clearly visible.

The land adjoining the holy well was owned by the Knights Templars in the 12th century —— an interesting reminder of the days when knights bearing the traditional red cross were influential in Europe.

There is huge interest in the site of Holy Wells generally at the present time, and people in Whitnash are understandably keen to have the well site made generally accessible, which it is not at the present. It is the dream of many in Whitnash to achieve this, and perhaps in time for the millenium celebrations, something can be organised?

ANCIENT ROADS AND FIELD NAMES

It is often difficult to piece together the history of Celtic and early Saxon times and ancient road and field names often provide extremely important information for the historian.

The field which adjoins the holy well was once called Castle Hill Field and this would suggest that it was the site of a Hill Fort in Celtic times. Such forts were usually constructed on mounds and near the brook in the section named 'Castle Hill Furlong' prior to the enclosures, such a mound still exists despite repeated ploughing.

It is generally thought that Christianity spread to many places in England in Roman times and the existence of the ruins of a Roman Villa at Radford (at Pounce Hill, around half a mile from the site of the holy well) may have significance in this respect. If Christianity was spread in England via the Romans and such roads as the Fosse Way, it is quite conceivable that Whitnash could have possessed an early monastery or church.

To the south of the area now occupied by St Margaret's Church and the Rectory is a field once known as St Peter's Mount. This suggests that the land had a connection with a Church or monastery of that name, but there is no obvious connection to be made with an existing local church.

By around 600 A.D. a tribe of Anglo Saxons known as the Hwiccas occupied south Warwickshire and lands to the west and Whitnash was adjacent to the tribal border which afterwards became adopted as the diocesan boundary between Worcester and Lichfield in Christian times around 200 years later. Early Hwiccan Christian establishments were usually dedicated to St Peter and along the Whitnash boundary near Ashford Road and the Harbury Lane, there still exists a noticeable high bank and ditch which may well be the remains of some tribal or diocesan boundary.

If St Peter's Mount (now the site of church car park behind Watts Cottages) was the site of an earlier monastery or church, the fact that the land was high and provided a good vantage point with views beyond the Fosse Way would have made it an ideal site to defend. Old legends often have some degree of truth in them and this explanation would fit in with the account of an earlier church site as given by Burgess.

Besides the ley line already mentioned, several ancient roads encircle and cross Whitnash territory —— the Fosse Way serving as the southern boundary to the town. Sections of this road near Leamington are said to be ancient tracks, merely improved and linked together by the Romans. The western boundary of Whitnash is on or near the Harbury Lane which may well have been a saltway between Warwick and Wormleighton and was known in past centuries as the Itchington Road.

The bridle path to Radford Semele which now goes down Church Lane and has two right angles on the Radford side of the brook was once known as a "Regia Via" —— an important road in medieval times, the name perhaps corresponding to a main road or 'high street' today. Also a road from St Margaret's Church (or perhaps St Peter's Mount nearby) which followed part of the course of the present Golf Lane to the Fosse Way was known as a Ridgeway. The Golf Lane area lies adjacent to a geological fault known as 'The Whitnash Fault' where the Liassic Clays and limestone found east of The Fosse are predominant, instead of the older Mercia Mudstone found in Leamington, and it seems possible this ancient road followed the fault line.

On maps several centuries old, a house of some size is marked near Castle Hill Field and the present Golf Lane hill (up the bridle path past Fieldgate Lane) was once known as Grange Hill, suggesting a settlement existed near there in times past, for the word 'grange' can mean hamlet. Also near upper Golf Lane there was once a field known as Old Town Meadow again suggesting that there was once an earlier settlement near the Fosseway.

Many early convents had granges (country houses with outbuildings) on their outlying estates and if there ever was a convent or monastery on St Peter's Mount, such a grange could have been near the Fosse Way.

For information concerning recent archaeological discoveries and for identification of the pottery found at the site of the Holy Well, I am indebted to Philip Wise, Keeper of Archaeology, based at the Warwickshire Museum in the Market Place in Warwick. For those readers who would like to know more about the early history of Whitnash and conduct further investigations themselves, the books I used are listed in the Bibliography. In addition, an annotated copy of this book is placed in the Warwickshire County Record Office giving the numbers of the documents to which I refer.

ST MARGARET'S CHURCH AND SOME OF ITS RECTORS

When Christianity was struggling to overcome pagan beliefs in England around 600 A.D., Pope Gregory 1 suggested that wherever possible churches should be built on sites of pagan significance. So it seemed to be with Whitnash, for it is generally accepted that the artificial mound on which the present church, rectory and surroundings are situated was an ancient British earthwork of some kind.

In addition ,like some other ancient churches, Whitnash is not built exactly East to West but is set at a slight angle, seemingly in alignment with something more ancient than the rays of the rising sun on the appointed day of the patron saint.

Until January 1960 an ancient elm tree stood in front of the church —— this tree almost certainly being older than the 15th century tower and possibly older than 800 years. From old illustrations the tree would seem to have once been a pollard elm and in his book "Trees and Woodland in an English Landscape" Oliver Rackham writes,

"Of special interest are the ancient trees of settlements. Gnarled elm pollards are a characteristic feature of many villages and hamlets ....There are many different kinds of settlement elms which once introduced are almost impossible to get rid of, and maintain their distinctive characters for ever by suckering. It has been claimed that some of these elms were brought from the Continent by Bronze and Iron Age men".

During 1959, a vociferous campaign was launched to try to prevent the demolition of the ancient elm, but in the end the Parish Council had its way and the village green was "tidied up" and rid of its settlement elm. Even today the value of ancient trees is not realised and simply because the tree was hollow and a target for courting couples and naughty choirboys, it was considered an eyesore by some.

Like around 200 other ancient parish churches in England, Whitnash Church is dedicated to St Margaret of Antioch, a somewhat legendary figure who was popular before the Norman Conquest. She is the patron saint of women in childbirth and she is generally portrayed with a cross in her hands and a dragon beneath her feet, for legends told how she was tortured and swallowed by a dragon. In the present church building there are numerous examples of carved daisies (marguerites) for these are generally accepted as one of the emblems of St Margaret. Also several stained glass windows, notably one in the porch,

THIS PENCIL SKETCH OF A PICTURESQUE VILLAGE GREEN IS DATED 1819. Green Farm is shown on the left and the half-timbered Glebe House is to the right of the church. The rather ramshackle building to the right of the ancient elm tree is the blacksmith's shop ——-a most necessary service in the days of horse transport. For years this drawing lay in the attic of Green Farm and it has been lent to me by Marjorie Marriott (née Masters) who lived in the farmhouse until the 1930s. (MM))

depict St Margaret with a cross and dragon.

In all probability, a wooden Saxon church first stood on this site and in the 12th century this was rebuilt. Around 1121 Lesceline, the widow of Humfrey of Hasculf Musard who was the ruler of Whitnash in the time of Domesday in 1086, gave the church to Nostell Priory in Yorkshire ——an Augustinian House. However in 1122 Kenilworth Priory, another Augustinian house, was established and Lesceline subsequently granted the advowson of Whitnash Church to that Priory which retained it until the Reformation. After that time, the right to appoint the Rector remained with the crown until it was purchased by Lord Leigh of Stoneleigh in 1615.

During the reign of Henry 1 (1100 -1135) when a new building was erected on the site, 18 acres of land were given to the church and thus the Whitnash Rector was supplied with a reasonable income. Also in the days when a tithe (tenth) of all crops in the parish was payable to the church, a Rector had the right to all, as opposed to a vicar who kept only a proportion of the tithes. So to be appointed Rector of Whitnash was to be appointed to a position of local power and wealth.

A fuller description of the history of the church was given in a previous booklet, but it is interesting to note that when the Church was restored and partly rebuilt from 1855 -

THE ANCIENT WHITNASH ELM, HOLLOW WITH AGE AND PERHAPS AS MUCH AS 800 YEARS OLD CAN BE SEEN CLEARLY IN THIS 1959 PHOTOGRAPH. Sadly the old elm was removed in January 1960 but there are several pieces of its bark still carefully preserved. (Photograph courtesy of the Leamington Evening Telegraph)

1880, various ancient items were found including a section of 'herringbone' Saxon stonework, an unusual window which had never been glazed and a small piscina and sedile. Some of these items may well have dated from the reign of Henry 1, if not earlier.

The tower of the church was built in the late 15th century and it is now the oldest part of the church. Behind a protective cover, the original strap-hinge door to the tower still exists ———this unrestored item for me evoking a strong atmosphere of centuries past. It seems extremely likely that the tower was built by Benedict Medley, Lord of the Manor who died in 1503, whose brass and that of his wife is now on the south wall of the chancel. An important man in his day, Benedict and his wife were buried in the chancel and their brasses are considered amongst the finest in Warwickshire.

Another fine brass in the chancel is that of Richard Bennet, Rector from 1492 to 1534, who probably conducted the burial services for the Medleys and was the first (or second) Rector to use the tiny door to the tower.

The churchyard has several interesting items, in particular a famous stone to a 20 year old virgin who died of a broken heart in 1725. Also until around 20 years ago, there was a memorial to "John Meads, for many years Open Field Shepherd of this Parish who died Feb. 12th 1865".

THIS TYPICAL PORTRAYAL OF ST MARGARET OF ANTIOCH SHOWS HER CARRYING A CROSS WHILST A DRAGON LIES AT HER FEET. Carved in ebony by Agnes Bonham, this design was used on the cover of a prayer book first used in St Margaret's Church at Easter 1867. (GC)

(Reproduced by permission of Warwickshire County Record Office)

Rectors

There have been some famous Rectors in Whitnash over the centuries. Although from Medieval times onward Whitnash was a smallish village, it was larger than Leamington until the late 18th century and was considered a beautiful and healthy rural retreat.

In 1609 Nicholas Greenhill became Rector of Whitnash, having previously been one of the early Headmasters of Rugby School from 1602 -1605. Nicholas Greenhill was Rector for over 40 years and on the wall of the chancel is a famous and witty memorial to him beginning "This Greenhill periwigd with snow". An interesting reference to him was contained in a book about Radford Semele written in 1976 by Rev. L. Parsons. Nicholas Greenhill had witnessed the will and afterwards appraised the goods of Rev. Richard Gardiner, Vicar of Radford Semele who died in 1631. Richard Gardiner's will included the rather touching request *"I give unto Mr Greenhill of Whitnash the few books he has of mine, and unto Mrs Greenhill I give my harp".*

The Rector of Whitnash from 1660 to 1674 was Dr Thomas Holyoake, the son of Francis Holyoake, Rector of Southam. During the Civil War Thomas fought for the king and commanded a company of foot soldiers in Oxford. After Oxford surrendered, Thomas became a doctor but in 1660 at the Restoration, Lord Leigh made him Rector of Whitnash in gratitude for his war service. Like his father who compiled a dictionary which he helped to complete, Thomas was buried in St Mary's Church, Warwick.

In the chancel of St Margaret's is a rather sad memorial to Thomas Morse (Rector of Whitnash from 1732 to 1784) and his family. After listing the names of Thomas' wife Ann, their four sons and three daughters who all died childless, the marble inscription ends, *"Friendly regard has inscribed this marble in memory of a family now totally extinct".*

Thomas Morse had also been Rector of Ashow and like many places in England in the late 18th and early 19th century, after his death Whitnash had no resident Rector for around 60 years. Services were taken by other clerics from nearby parishes, although officially there was a Rector living elsewhere.

With no resident Rector, the church and Glebe House, the official residence of the Cleric, gradually slid into decay. By 1840 the church was in desperate need of restoration, having been propped up in various places, because the chancel walls were leaning outward around 18 inches.

THE WATER MILL AND LORDS OF THE MANOR

THE WATER MILL

The uneven field alongside the brook on the north-eastern side was traditionally known as Mill Dam Field and in medieval times there was a great dam across the brook, creating a huge mill pond which provided the power to operate at least one corn mill.

Historical documents describe how in 1279 the property held by the Lord of a Manor in Whitnash included a watermill with a great pool and in 1338 a mill and land was granted to Kenilworth Priory. We know that one end of the dam was on the Radford bank, for rent was payable in the 13th century for this privilege.

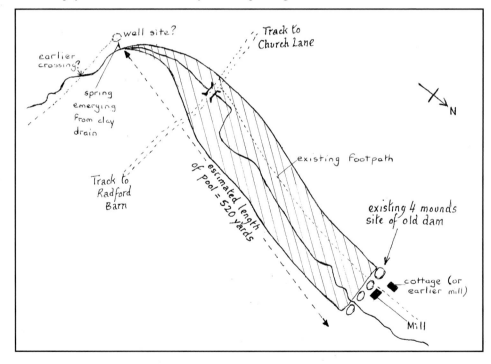

'THE GREAT POOL' IS ESTIMATED TO HAVE BEEN NEARLY A THIRD OF A MILE LONG. This sketch map of the area in medieval times shows the huge extent of the pool which probably gave rise to the nickname "Whitnash on the Ocean". An exit stream from the pool would have flowed past the mill. (Line drawing by Ian Box after an original sketch by D.T.N. Booth of Halesowen).

THIS ARTIST'S IMPRESSION SHOWS THE WATER MILL AND ADJACENT MILLER'S COTTAGE AS IT PROBABLY WAS IN MEDIEVAL TIMES. Based upon direct observation of the existing mounds, the low half timbered buildings would have had thatched roofs. The wooden launder carried water to the top of the wheel shaft and the miller would have used the simple bridge to cross the stream when he needed to get at the outer bearing of the waterwheel shaft, which would have needed regular greasing. (Line drawing by local author, artist and lecturer Rosemary Booth after an original sketch by D.T.N. Booth of Halesowen)

From various maps and archives I discovered that for the last 200 years at least, the area of the old mill and dam in the water meadow had not been cultivated, but had been classed as waste ground, used only for summer grazing of cattle and the harvesting of "withy tops" ——willow for basket making.

In 1993 the 'Whitnash Society' contacted Mr D.T.N. Booth of Halesowen, a member of the Midland Wind and Watermills Group and author of a book on Midland Watermills. Tim Booth subsequently revisited the site and made a report. In it he described

"a substantial dam which still stands to a considerable height, despite being out of use for at least three hundred years.....When in use the dam would have held back a a very large amount of water, creating the 'great pool' of Whitnash Mill referred to in early documents. This pool would certainly have extended as far upstream as the bridge on the track between Church Lane and Radford Barn and quite possibly into the fields to the south.

Of great interest is what appears to be an ancient watercourse leaving the brook a short distance north of the bridge....

It is most unusual to be able to study a site which ceased development over three hundred years ago and retains some features which can be dated to the 13th century with

16

*THE MEMORIAL BRASSES TO BENEDICT MEDLEY AND HIS WIFE ARE CONSIDERED
TO BE AMONGST THE FINEST IN WARWICKHIRE. Benedict, who was Lord of the Manor
of Whitnash and Clerk of the Signet to King Henry V11, died in 1503 and was buried in the
chancel of St Margaret's Church. (Reproduced by permission of Warwickshire County Record
Office)*

certainty whilst others may be as far back as the 11th century."

Both Mr Booth and I thought it was quite conceivable that the great mill pool gave rise to the nickname *"WHITNASH ON THE OCEAN"* which still exists to this day. *'Whitnash situated on the large expanse of water'* would have seemed a suitable reference in medieval times and it is amazing how names persist in rural areas.

As the Mill Dam Field has been undisturbed for centuries, it is interesting from the point of view of plants. Enthusiasts from the Warwickshire Wildlife Trust have inspected the site, which has barely been touched for 30 years, and it is hoped to complete a survey of birds, animals and plants. Adjoining the Mill Dam Field is an ox-bow lake and Pebble Island, traditionally the playground of the young for generations and now a famous beauty spot. Kingfishers and otters have been spotted in the area and today the secluded path through the meadow is a favourite walk for many from Whitnash and Radford ——-just as it has been for centuries.

LORDS OF THE MANOR

We are apt to forget that in centuries past the Lord of the Manor had enormous power in each village. The manor house was almost always situated close to the parish church and the local people were locked into a rigid class system headed by the Lord of the Manor. After the Norman Conquest in 1066 land was granted to Norman over-lords who in turn rented out the manors and villages for which they had no need.

The overlord of Whitnash in 1086 was Humfrey of Hasculf Musard and this family continued to hold the overall rights for centuries; land in Leamington Hastings and Haseley also being in the same ownership. In 1346 Thomas Savage of Tachbrook Mallory was in possession of the manor and in 1483 his descendent sold it to Benedict Medley of Warwick.

To confuse what seems to be a complicated land holding system even further, in many villages there were several manors and so it was with Whitnash.

Benedict Medley (c1450 -1503) was a well known figure in the later 15th century and he was a member of the household of George Duke of Clarence.(This nobleman was brother of King Edward 1V and he probably met his death drowned in a butt of Malmesey wine!)

Benedict was given the official position of Clerk of the Signet by King Henry V11 and he and his family had many connections with Warwick and Warwickshire.

In 1483 Benedict purchased one manor in Whitnash from Thomas Savage, Tachbrook Mallory in 1496 and another manor in Whitnash from Sir Henry Willoughby in 1499. It is believed that it was Benedict Medley who was responsible for building the tower of St Margaret's and on their death, both he and his second wife Agnes Govis were buried in the chancel.

For much of this information concerning the Medley family I am indebted to a pamphlet in Warwickshire County Record Office compiled by a modern descendant of the Medleys. This booklet suggested that Benedict, his sons and later his grandsons occupied the Whitnash, Tachbrook and Warwick lands, but the main branch of the family was in Essex.

It is known that Robert Medley (grandson of Benedict) occupied the Whitnash Manor

THE HALF-TIMBERED FRAMEWORK BELOW THE GABLE CAN JUST BE SEEN IN THIS DELIGHTFUL SUMMER SNAP OF THE MANOR HOUSE TAKEN IN THE LATE 1930s. (FG)

House and on his death in 1547 he left a sum of money to buy a bell for the church. Robert's son Henry died in 1578 and in 1604 his grandson sold the Whitnash Manor.

By 1800 much land in Whitnash had been bought by the Earl of Warwick and as late as 1936 the Earl was listed as the largest landowner in Whitnash.

In 1826 Henry Eyres Landor (the brother of the famous writer Walter Savage Landor) bought the Manor House near the Church and acquired four other farms which had once belonged to ancestors of his mother, Elizabeth Savage of Tachbrook. From 1826 to his death in 1868, the wealthy H.E. Landor was a most worthy Lord of the Manor. In his later life he lived in Savage's House in Tachbrook, but although he rented out the Manor House and the other property, he took a great interest in Whitnash, amongst other things endowing the school with land and money in 1860. H.E. Landor gave many items to the church and when a subscription list was raised to help someone in distress, he always made a generous donation. H.E. Landor left his Whitnash property to Sophy Landor, his niece, and the title of Lord of the Manor remained with the descendants of the Landor family until the mid 20th century.

From information already mentioned, it will have become clear that there was at least one other manor in Whitnash, besides that adjacent to the church and there may have been as many as three manors at one time.

The Manor House

Being situated close to the medieval church, it would appear that this was the main manor house (if indeed any other existed) and it was generally known as such.

THIS ELEGANT DRAWING ROOM IN THE MANOR HOUSE WAS PHOTOGRAPHED IN THE LATE 1930s. (FG)

WHAT A TRAGEDY IT WAS THAT THIS 17TH CENTURY HOUSE
WAS LOST TO WHITNASH! THIS JOINTED CRUCK TRUSS ON A
UPSTAIRS LANDING IN THE MANOR HOUSE PROBABLY INDI-
CATED THAT THE HOUSE HAD ONCE HAD AN OPEN HALL. This
photograph was taken shortly before demolition.(IB)

Partly constructed in the 17th century, this timber framed house was a most interesting building. It had five bedrooms, apart from the attics and a useful cellar. During the 19th century it was modernised and extended, but the upstairs landings still contained huge beams suggesting that the house had once had an open hall, which was later split up into different levels and rooms.

In the 19th and 20th centuries large glasshouses occupied much space in the garden adjacent to the house and although the house was demolished in 1959, part of the garden wall still remains.

NEAT FLOWER GARDENS AND EXTENSIVE GLASSSHOUSES STRETCHED AWAY BEYOND THE MANOR HOUSE IN THE LATE 1930s. Frances Gibbs, who worked at the house at the time and also lent me this photograph, described recently how the glasshouses were filled with chrysanthemums and tomatoes, which were then sold. Although the Manor House and garden were demolished over 35 years ago, much of the boundary wall shown here still remains. (FG)

THE LIFE AND TIMES OF CANON YOUNG

When Rev. James Reynolds Young became Rector in 1846, life in Whitnash, as in the rest of England, was just about to change. Born in London in 1807 , James Young was educated at Charterhouse School (where he became friendly with fellow student W.M. Thackeray) and Caius College Cambridge. Wealthy and well connected, in many ways he was typical of some Rectors in Victorian times who gave unstintingly of their own time and money to their parishioners.

SOMETIMES IT SEEMS DIFFICULT TO COMPREHEND A TIME WHEN CANON YOUNG WORE A TALL HAT LIKE THIS ROUND WHITNASH! Rector, teacher, printer, botanist ——he was a most charismatic and talented man. (By permission of Denbighshire Record Office and Ms Judy Corbett)

EDITH MARY, SHOWN HERE IN A PHOTOGRAPH TAKEN AROUND 1865,
WAS THE ELDEST CHILD OF CANON YOUNG AND HIS WIFE MARY ANN.
Born in 1848, Edith together with her three sisters and four brothers must have
been quite friendly with the pupils at the exclusive preparatory school run at
Whitnash Rectory. Indeed this photograph comes from an album compiled by the
mother of one of the pupils.
(By permission of Denbighshire Record Office and Ms Judy Corbett)

However, Rev. Young was not typical in the fact that he achieved a huge amount in his lifetime and in many respects became quite well known. He seemed to possess huge charisma and had liberal ideas well ahead of his time in many ways.

A School For the Sons of the Nobility

When Canon Young arrived in Whitnash, the population of the village was less than 350. The ancient church was falling down and the old Glebe House in sad need of modernisation. His first task was to build a new Rectory in 1847 and he chose a fine site nearby, with views over the parish to the Fosse Way. His wife Mary Ann bore 8 children in 10 years ——Edith Mary born 1848, William Henry born 1849, Ruth Isobel born 1850, Charles James born 1851, Edward Annesley born 1853, Walter Kershaw born 1854, Margaret Alice born 1856 and Nora Sophy born 1857.

In 1851 at his new Rectory, Canon Young began a boarding school for boys around the ages of 8 to 14, and places at Whitnash became much sought after. The school was very exclusive, with perhaps a dozen pupils at most at any one time and many of the boys were sons of the nobility. For example listed amongst the pupils in 1851 were the Earl of Dunmore and Lord Brabazon. Between 1851 and 1870 a whole succession of boys including Lord Adare (the 4th Earl of Dunraven in 1871), Arthur Smith Barry (Lord Barrymore in 1902), Hon. Ivo Vesey (4th Viscount de Vesci in 1875), William Wentworth Watson (whose family seat was Rockingham Castle in Northants) and many more attended Whitnash. Of particular interest to historians are the pupils Herbert Maxwell, later a Baronet, author and distinguished M.P. and his friend Charles Salisbury Mainwaring, the son of the heiress of Galltfaenan Estate in North Wales. In 1932 Sir Herbert Maxwell's autobiography entitled "Evening Memories" was published in which he wrote much about his happy times when at Whitnash and the Mainwaring family kept a wonderful album of photographs (including many of Whitnash) which is

THIS PENSIVE FACE BELONGED TO CHARLES CECIL COTES ——-ONE OF THE PUPILS AT WHITNASH RECTORY SCHOOL FROM 1855 TO 1859. Like many of the other boys, Charles Cotes continued his education at Eton School and Oxford University and in later life he became an M.P., being a junior Lord of the Treasury in Gladstone's ministry of 1880. He owned Woodcote and the picturesque half-timbered Pitchford House in Shropshire. (By permission of Denbighshire Record Office and Ms Judy Corbett)

now in Denbighshire Record Office at Ruthin.

Herbert Maxwell painted a glowing picture of the school at Whitnash in 1855. He wrote,

"It was Warwickshire in full flush of spring ——-elms in a mist of tender greenery, rich pasture land surrounding a pretty brick-built parsonage, a grey towered church, and a village of houses timbered black and white, with more trees than houses along the straggling street....I shared a bedroom with Alfred Duncombe, son of the Dean of York.....During the winter we used to attend dancing classes in Leamington, and even now the smell of new kid gloves brings to mind the graceful figure, sunny hair and pervenche -blue eyes of the Hon. Fanny Butler......In one respect Whitnash must have been in advance of other schools of that period in the encouragement and facilities which we enjoyed to interest our ourselves in natural history and country life. Each of us had a plot of garden ground..."

Printing

Canon Young was most interested in new aspects of study such as science, nature study and languages. He was fascinated by printing and he installed a large machine at the Rectory. His pupils used to assist him (also a professional printer on his day off from the "Leamington Spa Courier") and soon all kinds of printed matter was being produced at Whitnash, including some of the earliest parish magazines in the country in 1859.

Recently I have been privileged to examine a most rare and beautiful book, which was printed at Whitnash in 1871. It is a fascinating collection of the Recitations which the pupils of Canon Young used to perform each Christmas and not only does it include such items as the names of all the pupils and the term marks they obtained, it prints in full the

THIS PHOTOGRAPH SHOWS WHITNASH RECTORY AS IT WAS IN THE DAYS OF CANON YOUNG. The building on the left known as "The Cottage" was demolished around 1936 and the Rectory itself was demolished in 1959. However part of the terrace walls shown in the foreground still remain in the gardens of bungalows in Church Close. (ML)

*TAKEN AROUND THAT TIME, THIS EXCELLENT PHOTOGRAPH SHOWS
ST MARGARET'S CHURCH AS IT WAS OVER 130 YEARS AGO WHEN THE
INDUSTRIAL EXHIBITION IN WHITNASH TOOK PLACE IN JULY 1865.*
*The old elm, previously pollarded, had been allowed to develop naturally, the
church gates were made of metal and part of the old Glebe House was visible
behind the elm.*
(By permission of Denbighshire Record Office and Ms Judy Corbett)

poem or translation they recited. The book says a lot about Canon Young for on the second page the dedication reads

"To my young fellow workmen at the Whitnash Press this collection of our joint labours in past years is affectionately dedicated by their old friend J.R.Y."

Even if he had not been a sympathetic Rector often helping his poor villagers, or a talented teacher, or excellent organiser obtaining the best architect to rebuild the church, Canon Young might have been remembered as a keen amateur printer, whose works are much collected.

The Rebuilding of Whitnash Church

The restoration of the Whitnash Church had become an urgent matter, for the chancel walls were bulging outwards by 14 inches each side and Rev. Young engaged the services of one of the principal architects of his time (Sir) George Gilbert Scott. He drew up plans for the rebuilding of the chancel and work began in 1855. As work proceeded, certain ancient items were discovered such as a window never glazed, an old piscina and sedile and these and many other old items such as the three old brasses were resited in their original positions.

Francis Skidmore, a famous metal worker based in Coventry, who often worked with Scott, completed several items such as a new communion rail, a new communion cup cleverly copied from the Bennett brass and various stands and candelabra. Top quality

THIS WAS HOW THE INTERIOR OF ST MARGARET'S CHURCH LOOKED AROUND 1865. The old box-pews, erected in 1795, were soon to be replaced and the chancel, recently rebuilt and refurbished with 24 seats, often had 33 members of Canon Young's household (including pupils and guests) trying to squeeze in! At this time the church was illuminated by candles and around the newly erected pulpit can be seen various candelabra made by Francis Skidmore, the celebrated Coventry craftsman.
(By permission of Denbighshire Record Office and Ms Judy Corbett)

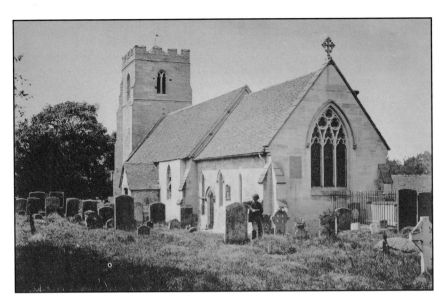

THE REAR OF ST MARGARET'S CHURCH AROUND 1865 WHEN THE SOUTH AISLE HAD NOT BEEN BUILT AND THE OLD PORCH WAS STILL IN PLACE. The tombs protected by railings (to deter grave robbers?) are those of the Eyres family —— from whom the writer Walter Savage Landor and his brother Henry Eyres Landor, Lord of the Manor of Whitnash, were descended.
(By permission of Denbighshire Record Office and Ms Judy Corbett)

Minton tiles were placed along the East wall and a new organ made by Walker and Co. of London was purchased.

The money for many of these items came of course from the parents of Canon Young's pupils ———he kept a careful list and wrote various descriptions of the church in which the patrons were given the credit. Naturally the parents (and grandparents) were pleased to contribute as their sons worshipped weekly in the building so the new chancel was furnished extremely well with top quality items.

The organ is interesting as it was installed in 1857 at the expense of Edward Wood of Newbold Revel, originally of Porthill, Burslem, who paid £140 to J.W. Walker & Sons of London (one of the foremost organ makers) for the stock instrument with six manual stops, one preparation and a 12 note pedal Bourdon. Mr Wood's son Edward attended the Rectory School from 1856 onwards and the organ was first played on October 29th 1857, the boy's birthday. After being extended various times and moved once or twice, the organ was rebuilt in 1994/5 by the firm of Hill, Norman and Beard of Norwich. When the organ builders removed pipes and other parts, certain pieces such as leather bellows and carpet packing were still the original items installed in 1857. After having had around £60,000 spent on it, the top quality instrument sounds magnificent today.

For the information on the 1857 instrument, I am indebted to the Archives Section of J.W. Walker and Sons Ltd. of Brandon, Suffolk.

In 1862 a new pulpit was constructed ———the carving done by a young amateur,

THE RECTORY DRIVE IN THE 1860s WAS TEEMING WITH ACTIVITY! The half-timbered Glebe House can just be seen to the left of the church tower. Today this drive, little altered, forms the roadway of Church Close. (Reproduced by permission of Warwickshire County Record Office)

Agnes Bonham, who was a friend of the Landor family and the Rector. She completed several items in the church including the wall panels either side of the altar and some of the carved capitals. Her work was exceptionally fine and she also carved the ebony cover shown on page 12.

In 1867 the new South Aisle was added and also the porch, largely paid for by some members of Magdalen College Oxford, who had connections with Whitnash Church. The money for the rebuilding of the nave was rather harder to raise for, by then, parishioners were rather tired of contributions and the school had been given up. However, it was a triumphal day in 1880 when it was opened and the rebuilt and restored church was complete.

The Coming of the Railway and Field Enclosures

Whitnash was extremely late in having the open strip fields enclosed—— the agreement for Leamington was made in 1767 and that for Radford Semele in 1716 , but the award for Whitnash was not completed until 1850. By that time the route for the Great Western Railway to Leamington and Birmingham had been planned and preliminary work begun.

For over 3 years 5,000 men laboured to open the Railway line from Oxford to Birmingham, which ran straight through the parish of Whitnash. As in Harbury, it was necessary to dig a deep cutting in Whitnash and 350,000 cubic yards of earth had to be displaced ——some of which was no doubt used to form the embankments necessary in the south of Whitnash. After the cutting was dug, a bridge was necessary to allow access to fields near to the brook. "Black Bridge" was placed at the bottom of Church Lane and it soon became a congregating point for the youth of the village.

"LORD OF THE ISLES" WAS PROBABLY THE MOST FAMOUS BROAD GAUGE LOCOMOTIVE OF ALL AND SHE SHOULD HAVE HAULED THE FIRST OFFICIAL TRAIN TO PASS THROUGH WHITNASH. However she did not do so as she was involved in a slight collision south of Banbury and the G.W.R. Directors' Special train was much delayed. Later she did pass through Whitnash, once hauling the Royal Train with Queen Victoria and Prince Albert aboard. She had no cab for the driver and the only brakes were blocks on one side of the tender. (Photograph reproduced by permission of the Railway Museum, York)

I like to imagine the scene at Black Bridge as it might have been on September 30th 1852 when a crowd gathered around 11.45 a.m.to watch the first train, a Directors' Special from Paddington, hauled by the famous locomotive "Lord of the Isles". What mutterings and grumblings there must have been from the villagers when the minutes and hours passed and there was no train sight! Those in Whitnash and Leamington, where a special reception had been planned in the Regent Hotel, had no means of knowing that the train had run into the back of another at Aynho, outside Banbury, desite the fact that the famous Isambard Kingdom Brunel (Chief Engineer of the Great Western Railway) and Daniel Gooch (locomotive designer) were on the footplate, in addition to the driver. Eventually the train did pass through Whitnash —— more than 2 hours late and not hauled by "Lord of the Isles" but by a far older broad-gauge locomotive.

I must admit that I.K. Brunel is a particular hero of mine and I think it is most fitting that a road is Whitnash is named after him. When he eventually arrived at the large reception at the Regent Hotel, when asked to make a speech, Brunel declined, saying that what ever qualities the Directors thought he possessed, he never could make a speech and never would, preferring to undertake such tasks as he knew he could perform well! Needless to say Brunel sat down to great cheers!

Change, Hardship and Botany

It seems to me that it was as well for Whitnash and its inhabitants that it was Canon Young who presided over a very traumatic period in its history. Had the village had a less talented or sympathetic Rector, things might have been vastly different today.

When Canon Young came to Whitnash, the village was a sleepy place as described by the famous American writer Nathaniel Hawthorne. He visited several times in the 1850s and included a lengthy description of Whitnash in his book "Our Old Home" published in 1863 —— part of which reads,

"You soon find yourself in the heart of Whitnash, and see an irregular ring of rustic ancient dwellings surrounding the village green, on one side of which stands the church ....the church tower is mossy and much gnawed by time ...it thrills you with strange emotion to think that this little church of Whitnash, humble as it seems, stood for ages under the Catholic faith, and has not materially changed since Wickliffe's days and that it looked as gray as now in Bloody Mary's time, and that Cromwell's troopers broke off the stone noses of those same gargoyles that are now grinning in your face... The man who died yesterday or ever so long ago walks the street today, and chooses the same wife that he married a hundred years since, and must be buried again tomorrow under the same kindred dust that has already covered him half a score of times."

The Enclosures, the coming of the railway, the rise in size and popularity of Leamington must have been traumatic for the villagers and when the crops failed in the 1870s and poor people all over England were starving, Canon Young bought in rice from Liverpool —— subsidizing the price via a subscription list, so that the poor could afford to buy it. Lending Libraries, Evening Classes, Parties at the Rectory —— all these Canon Young organized for his parishioners and deservedly he and his family were locally popular.

However, one aspect of his life which particularly interests me is his work in the field of botany. Along with his friend Dr H. Baker and Henry Bromwich of Myton, Canon Young compiled notes and a herbarium —— the result being a "Catalogue of Plants Collected in Warwickshire in 1873". At this time the study of botany and science was not widespread and this early list mentions wild plants which were growing in Whitnash.

Canon Young died in 1884 and was buried in the churchyard —— surely he ranks as one of the most charismatic, hardworking and respected village Rectors of all time?

FOSSE FARM (NOW LEAMINGTON HALL FARM)

FOSSE FARM (NOW LEAMINGTON HALL FARM) WAS BUILT IN 1850 FOR HENRY EYRES LANDOR, THE LORD OF THE MANOR. Although the farm buildings have been sold off, the house itself still looks basically the same as it did in this snapshot taken in the 1950s. (IB)

One of the most interesting and least well known farm houses in Whitnash is that close to the Fosse Way, once known as Fosse Farm.

The old road from Whitnash to the Fosse seems to have passed close to the site of the house, but after the field enclosures of 1850 Henry Eyres Landor who owned the land built a new model farm on lines suggested by the latest planning. The new farm house was set slightly apart and the farm buildings were ranged on 3 sides of a courtyard.

In the early years the occupants of the house seemed dogged by misfortune. Henry Eyres Landor employed a farm bailiff who lived in the house and supervised the running of the farm and one of the early occupants was Mr Lane. Twin babies died in mysterious circumstances and in 1865 the uninsured threshing machine was destroyed by fire.

"A GIFTED DAUGHTER OF THE COUNTY" WAS HOW THE DAILY MIRROR DESCRIBED MAY STRETTON OF FOSSE FARM IN 1913. May became skilled in woodcarving and devoted much of her time to it, completing large carved tables, as well as smaller items. (AV)

From the 1890s the Stretton family were the tenants and May Stretton, one of the daughters, was a most talented individual. She became keen on woodcarving whilst in her teens and after taking lessons carved a number of items including a large table. In 1913 the Daily Mirror carried an article about her entitled "A Gifted Daughter of the County", together with photographs of items she had carved.

May would rise at 5a.m. and complete household duties until around 9 a.m. then she had time for her carving. She was very skilled in farming matters and at one time had an orphaned 3 year old shire horse which she had raised and kept as a pet. Like many at that time she rode to hunts and had three horses, Kit, Stella and Harkaway, which she often rode or drove. Eventually May married and moved away and later the farm was sold.

In the 1960s the owner of the farm was Welsh-born Fred Hawkins who also had a farm in North Devon. With the help of only one other assistant, Hartie Boyles, he farmed over 300 acres, employing tramps and other casual labour when available. Local boys would help him in the school holidays and they were amused to see Annie, his long-horned pet cow which followed him around!

Until the late 1960s the farm was approached via a track from Upper Golf Lane, but later a separate drive was made from the Fosse way. In the early 1990s the farm buildings were up for sale so that they could be turned into homes, but the actual farm house, which was sold separately some years previously seems to have changed very little . There is still a plaque high on the wall which commemorates the fact that the house was built by Henry Eyres Landor in 1850.

*AT ONE TIME MAJOR BONNIKSEN OWNED THE GARAGE AT THE
JUNCTION OF ST HELEN'S ROAD AND TACHBROOK ROAD AND
HE IS PICTURED HERE IN 1938 WITH A GIPSY MOTH AIRCRAFT IN
THE BACKGROUND.(GE)*

BONNIKSEN'S AERODROME

In the 1920s, Jack Ashton and his wife Nellie (the sister of nonagenarian Mrs Hilda Avis of Landor House) were renting Fosse Farm. Ex-RAF Squadron Leader, Major Julius E. Bonniksen of Leamington, who had learned to fly during the First World War, wanted to create a local aerodrome and in 1932 he was allowed to buy farmland adjoining the Harbury Lane for this purpose. Hedges and trees were felled and the ground was levelled in order to provide a suitable landing area for light aircraft.

Originally named the Royal Leamington Spa Aircraft Park and Flying Club, a bungalow was built for occupation by the owner and his family. A hangar for Major Bonnniksen's De Havilland Gipsy Moth aircraft was also built.

In 1934 the aerodrome was renamed the Leamington, Warwick and District Aero Club and it was registered as a company. The bungalow was partly converted into a Club House for members of the Flying Club and the original hangar was extended to accommodate four Gipsy Moth aircraft, a well equipped workshop and a viewing verandah. Dual instruction for club members was £2 per hour, solo flying being 35 shillings an hour.

The grass airfield was continually cropped short by sheep from Fosse Farm which were allowed to roam freely. Before flying could commence, the sheep had to be rounded up and enclosed for safety reasons!

In 1933 Sir Alan Cobham's National Aviation Day Circus gave a display and for a couple of days there were traffic jams along the Harbury Lane as numerous visitors tried to converge on the site. In the next few years Sir Alan Cobham made further visits as did C.W.A Scott and Campbell Black. Joy Flights during these displays started at 5 shillings a trip.

An amusing anecdote concerning the National Aviation Day Display in 1934 is provided by a bundle of letters in the Warwickshire County Record Office.

Evensong at St Margaret's Church on 24th June was disturbed by the noise of low

MAJOR BONNIKSEN (RIGHT) AND A GROUP OF INTERESTED SPECTATORS BESIDE A DE HAVILLAND GIPSY MOTH AIRCRAFT IN 1938.(GE)

flying aircraft, "the noise of the engines at times made it almost impossible for the congregation to hear the clergyman," wrote the churchwarden Mr Ashford in a letter of complaint. Eventually, after a whole series of letters, on 10th July 1934 Sir Alan Cobham himself wrote to Mr Ashford apologising for the interruption and explaining that worsening visibility and weather conditions had caused aircraft to fly lower than normal.

Flying continued until the outbreak of the Second World War in 1939 when all private flying ceased and the aircraft were impressed into the R.A.F. Two Bellman type hangars were erected in the early war years, plus outbuildings for use by the Sir W.G. Armstrong Whitworth Aircraft Company of Coventry for the servicing and repair of Whitley bombers. On one occasion an Ensign passenger aircraft made an emergency landing there but it ended up across the Harbury Lane and had to be dismantled before removal! Major Bonniksen was recalled to the R.A.F. as a flying instructor and he served in that capacity for the duration of the war.

Much of the first hand information included here came from Gordon Evans, once of Avon Road (where his parents kept an Off- Licence) and now resident in Southam. He said on leaving school in the early 1930s, after a short spell working at Lockheed, he went to the Flying Club as an apprentice ground engineer, eventually learning to fly under the Civil Air Guard Scheme before the outbreak of war. He described to me recently how he was still in touch with one of Major Bonniksen's daughters, both remembering those so called "golden days" of flying.

After the war, the aerodrome was sold and a variety of uses were found for the land and the buildings. At present, in 1996, Car Boot Sales and Go-Kart Races are held in the former wartime aircraft hangars, which are still recognisable, but the adjoining land has been given over to other purposes.

In 1992 Leamington Football Club bought some land close by for a new football field and this is now under grass, although the pitches are not yet ready for play.

I must say I find it most irritating that although quite clearly the airfield was in Whitnash, it has gone down in history as Bishops Tachbrook Airfield or that of Leamington Spa!

INTERESTING CHARACTERS OF THE 19th AND 20th CENTURIES

It goes without saying that it is the people who make village and town life what it is and in each century there have been charismatic leaders or unusual characters. Here are just two brief pen-portraits of interesting people and photographs of a few others.

MISER MURCOTT

Of all the strange tales concerning Whitnash that of the bizarre death of Miser Murcott in 1894 probably caused the most interest and speculation.

John Murcott came to Whitnash around 1864 and he set up as a farmer. Born in Hinckley, Leicestershire, he was of good education and had previously been a Doctor; indeed for a time he had been a surgeon at Stafford. Interested in Astronomy and with the top floor of his house adapted as an Observatory, he had once tried to buy a telescope owned by the then Rector Rev. A.H.M. Russell.

Although at one time he actually advertised in a local newspaper for a wife, it was said that all the time that he lived in Whitnash no man or woman had ever crossed the threshold of his house. His particular aversion to women was said to his having once been crossed in love. He trusted no one and as a test of honesty, he would leave coins in his barns for his labourers to find.

As the years went by his behaviour grew more peculiar and food was delivered once a week by a shop in Leamington to his house which was where Seekings' Nursery once stood, between Golf Lane and The Plough and Harrow. He became more and more miserly and when his hay ricks caught fire a few years before his death, he refused to pay for the beer drunk in the nearby "Plough and Harrow" by members of the Leamington Fire Brigade who had successfully extinguished the blaze.

He treated his workers very badly and in May 1894, Golby, a young labourer, had gone to the local Court to try to force John Murcott to pay back wages of nearly £2 which were owing to him.

The Court was sympathetic to the labourer and every day for two weeks P.C. Savage, the Whitnash Policeman, went to Murcott's house to try to serve the Court Ruling, but there was no sign of the farmer. Eventually the Court ordered that the house be broken into and a ghastly sight met the Police and the Rector at 4 p.m. on the afternoon of 13th June 1894.

All doors and windows in the house were bolted and barred, with sheets of perforated zinc outside to protect him from the numerous stones frequently thrown by locals.

"The Warwick Advertiser" of 16th June 1894 carried a graphic description of the terrible scene.

"Accustomed as the Police were to scenes of filth and disorder, the constable assures us that he has never before seen anything so repulsive... The offensive odour pervading the premises was simply abominable and the place was literally overrun with vermin....They found Mr Murcott lying on a filthy mattress; dirty sheets and blankets lying on the floor....the body was discoloured and presented a very emaciated appearance. Close by his side was an empty meat tin from which it is presumed that the deceased took his last earthly meal."

Other local papers carried similar descriptions of the sad tale, the "Leamington Spa Courier" mentioning that *"spritely insects predominated everywhere"* ——— presumably a reference to the room being alive with fleas!

No large sums of money were found although there was a cheque for £56 made out to himself against a local bank.

Possibly it was because John Murcott was so unpleasant to others that rumours circulated about his death. A labourer described how he had taken some food to the house two weeks previously and he had seen Murcott at the door with a sword in his hand. It was well known that Murcott had pistols and swords in the house as protection and speculation grew that he had died of fright when someone from his past life at Stafford Gaol caught up with him, having threatened him at the previous Village Wake.

Others said that he lived entirely on tinned food and sponge cakes and that because he kept a large amount of money in the house, he had been robbed and murdered.

The truth would appear to be rather sadder than that ——— a 73 year old miser had starved himself to death, but even to this day, over a century afterwards, there is much interest in the mysterious death of this eccentric bachelor.

ROBERT PALMER

During the 19th Century the wealthy Palmer family was very influential in Whitnash. In mid-Victorian times, William Palmer leased Home Farm for many years and it is said that the numerous visitors in this period included Royalty. Mrs Betty Adams (née Edwards now aged 89) recalled that her aunt Sally Edwards had worked as a nursemaid for some time at Home Farm. It seemed that no expense was spared and the family had lots of beautiful clothes and possessions.

It was always rumoured in Whitnash when I was a child in the 1940s that the Palmer family had lost all their money when Greenways Bank in Warwick crashed in 1887, but whatever was the cause, sometime in the late 1880s, the family moved out of Home Farm and went nearby to "The Homestead" (now known as "Elderfield").

In 1891 this picturesque, thatched farmhouse was home to William Palmer aged 59 who described himself as a retired famer. His wife Harriet was 49 and three daughters Hannah aged 22, Ada aged 18 and Alice aged 13 helped their mother with household duties. Three sons ——-Walter aged 26 who was a timekeeper with the L.N.W.R., Thomas aged 24 who was a dairyman and Robert aged 5 completed the family.

I DO NOT KNOW WHETHER ROBERT PALMER (TAD) SHOWN LEFT OR LOCAL FARMER HARRY MARKHAM OF MOLLINGTON HILL FARM POSED FOR THIS PHOTOGRAPH, BUT THIS 1930s SHOT COULD NOT HAVE BEEN MORE NATURAL. The two are standing close to Tad's cowshed near Glamis Cottage and the milk float, pulled by the faithful horse Dumpling, belonged to Harry. (Reproduced by permission of Warwickshire County Council, Department of Libraries and Heritage, Leamington Library) '

"THE HOMESTEAD" THE FORMER RESIDENCE OF ROBERT (TAD) PALMER WAS EXTENSIVELY RENOVATED AROUND 1959. In this photograph the thatch of the 17th century building is being replaced by a tiled roof. Today "Elderfield" as it was renamed is one of the most attractive houses in Whitnash.(WG)

The Palmer family remained at the Homestead until the mid 20th century. Thomas and later Robert carried on as dairymen, keeping cows and pigs, but one by one the family grew smaller as members moved away or died.

Eventually by the late 1930s, only Alice and Robert were left and by then "Tad", as he had become known, was a well known character. Alice or "Lally", as she was described to me recently by Betty Adams, kept house for Tad, rarely venturing out except on a Sunday when she would don her best dress and bonnet and taking Tad's arm would walk with him down Golf Lane to view their orchard and fields which adjoined their thatched house which still contained expensive linen, ornaments and silver.

When Alice died and Tad was left to cope alone, the previously spotless house gradually grew run down.

I remember Tad quite clearly. To the village children he seemed very grumpy as he would yell at us to "Gerroff" his five barred gate if we climbed it to peer in at some of his pigs. He was often seen going into Leamington in a horse and trap and occasionally he would offer a lift to some of the older village girls, who had known him for many years.

His horse was usually caked with mud and likewise his leather gaiters, but it was obvious that all his animals loved him. One Christmas Eve I was sent to his house to buy 2sh 6d worth of holly for he had several holly trees around 30 feet high in his garden. I had to wait whilst he fed the cows, pigs and horse and in the gathering dusk, I could see how the animals rushed over to him as he approached with a pail of food. Somehow I felt deceitful as I used the delay to peer in through the grimy windows of his house at the huge hams hanging from the ceiling in his ramshackle kitchen.

Eventually old Tad could no longer carry on his small farm and he went to live in a house in Leamington with only his faithful old English sheepdog, Bob, for company. He could be seen riding his bicycle round the district with old Bob lolloping along by his side but it seemed a sad end.

His half-timbered farm-house was tiled and renovated in 1959, but to this day can be seen the old wooden door in the wall where Tad used to walk from his garden to the stable and cowshed alongside Glamis Cottage. Some say that when the old house was cleared, the well in the garden was partially filled with antique clothes and other relics of more prosperous times. Certainly when Tad died in 1965 aged 78 he was buried in the family grave in Whitnash ——fittingly the last body to be laid to rest in the ancient churchyard, close to the church. He may have had difficulties and his farmyard may have been muddier than most, but at heart he was a well mannered gentleman——- especially to a 10 year old girl who has never forgotten how he went to great lengths to tie up the holly, very carefully making a handle of string so that her fingers would not get scratched.

MRS WEBB LIVED OPPPOSITE TO OLD WHITNASH SCHOOL AROUND 100 YEARS AGO AND SHE ACTED AS CLEANER FOR ST MARGARET'S CHURCH FOR SOME YEARS. I find this a remarkable photograph for Mrs Webb's face demonstrates great character and fortitude. (MW)

ALTHOUGH WHITNASH WAS A SMALLISH COMMUNITY IN THE 1920s IT MUST NOT BE SUPPOSED THAT THE YOUNG PEOPLE OF THE VILLAGE WERE NOT BEAUTIFUL AND FASHION-CONSCIOUS! *I find this photograph (taken around 1920) of the late Mrs Annie Smith (left) and her cousin most interesting. (MW))*

THESE FOUR GREAT CHARACTERS IN THE 1950s ARE (FROM THE LEFT) HARRY COX, JACK COTTERILL, ARCHIE EDWARDS AND 'TODDY' PARKER. *Harry Cox lived in Hall's Close having previously lived in The Barracks, Archie Edwards lived in Chapel Yard and 'Toddy' Parker lived in The Doglands. Jack Cotterill, whose family had lived in the picturesque half-timbered cottage near the Plough for several generations, walked daily during the Second World War to Warwick School where he worked as a groundsman.(Photograph courtesy of Leamington Spa Courier)*

42

THE PEOPLE IN THIS GROUP WERE ALL TEACHERS AT WHITNASH SCHOOL.
Photographed near the old school (now St Margaret's Church Centre) in the early 1950s
from left to right the back row is ? possibly a student, Mrs Ingram and Mrs Maycock and
the front row is Mrs Nichols, Mrs Jones (headmistress who later became Mrs Rogers) and
Mrs Lambert. (IM)

THREE VERY POPULAR CHARACTERS OF THE 1990s —— DOCTORS PETER DAVIS (CENTRE), RICHARD DUNN AND JOHN EMERY (RIGHT) ARE PICTURED OUTSIDE THEIR BRUNSWICK STREET SURGERY IN 1995. Built around 1957, the Brunswick Street premises were first used as living accommodation and consulting rooms by Dr O'Connor who died suddenly in 1964. Doctors Doreen and David Bull of Radford Road, Leamington took over the practice in 1965 and they retired in 1984. In the same year the Coppice Road surgery was opened with a view to extending it as a main health centre within 15 years. 1995 actually saw the completion of this plan and today the new premises are much admired. (Photograph courtesy of Leamington Spa Courier)

44

MANY WILL RECOGNISE AVON ROAD RESIDENT FRANCES GIBBS, SEEN HERE WITH HER LATE HUSBAND BOB IN 1950. Exceptionally well known in Whitnash for her helpfulness and work with the Methodist Church, Frances received the Royal Maundy Money in Coventry Cathedral in Holy Week 1995, as did George Pratt, previously organist at St Margaret's Church for 50 years.(FG)

GEORGE BILLINGTON OF FRANKLIN ROAD HAS AN INTERESTING HOBBY —-THAT OF MAKING MATCHSTICK MODELS. 81 year old George and his wife Olive have lived in Franklin Road for nearly 60 years and in recent years they have been much connected with the Bowls Section of Whitnash Sports and Social Club. George's family home was in South Leamington and when young, he and his brother Ted used to sing in St Margaret's church choir in the 1920s. (Photograph courtesy of Leamington Spa Courier)

IN APRIL 1989 JEAN CLARKSON (NÉE BILLINGTON) WAS HONOURED FOR HER 25 YEARS SERVICE AS BROWN OWL TO THE LOCAL BROWNIE PACK WHEN CLARKSON DRIVE WAS NAMED AFTER HER. Jean is pictured in 1989 with some of her Brownies —— (left to right) the back row is Lisa Reading, Helen Pike, and Jenny Morgan. The front row is Susie Hill, Tracy Clearly, Abigail Hill and Victoria Timms. Now over 7 years later Jean is still Brown Owl! (Photograph courtesy of Observer Newspapers)

MICHAEL MORRIS HAS HAD A LONG AND DISTINGUISHED CAREER AS A LOCAL COUNCILLOR, HAVING SERVED ON WHITNASH TOWN COUNCIL, WARWICK RURAL DISTRICT COUNCIL AND THE COUNTY COUNCIL. He is pictured here whilst Mayor of Whitnash in July 1994 together with Susan Duane the Whitnash Carnival Queen. (Photograph courtesy of Observer Newspapers)

A SPORTING MISCELLANY

There is no way that I can include a complete history of all the various sporting achievements in Whitnash over the years, but I hope readers will find these few photographs and the two short accounts interesting. The first account concerns the village football team nearly 90 years ago and as you will read, the game was taken very seriously in those days. My information was gleaned from various copies of local newspapers of the year 1908 which are now in the Warwickshire County Record Office.

FOOTBALL ——— THE CUP RUNS OF 1908
Early in 1908 in the second round of the Southam Charity Cup, Whitnash were drawn away to Tachbrook but both that match and the replay at Whitnash were drawn. A third match had to be staged on neutral territory and this was played at Southam on 7th March 1908.

The Whitnash team was Horley in goal, Thacker and Richards as backs, Reading, Grubb, and E. Golby as half-backs and Horley, Woodward, Golby, Page and Owen as forwards. After 15 minutes Woodward headed a clever goal for Whitnash, but Tachbrook soon equalised. Then Woodward scored again for Whitnash and although Tachbrook pressed hard after half time, the Whitnash defence was magnificent! A large crowd had assembled to watch the match (no doubt many had travelled from Whitnash by bicycle or foot) and the Leamington Courier of 13th March reported that both teams gave the proceeds of the gate to local charities.

In the semi-final, Whitnash played Stockton away and again there was a large crowd. However, after just a few minutes forward E. Horley was injured and Whitnash had to play for the rest of the match with only ten men as there were no substitutes allowed in those days. At half-time Stockton were two goals up after employing "forcing tactics" but in the second half Whitnash had the slope in their favour and "a fine bout of passing ended in Page scoring". Just five minutes from time, Whitnash scored again and so earned a replay at home.

What a day the 28th March 1908 must have been in Whitnash! There was a large attendance (many of the 500 or so Whitnash inhabitants were probably there) but once again tragedy struck the Whitnash team. Richards, one of the best defenders in the team, "received a nasty kick" and was unable to continue. Once again the ten men played like heroes and at the end of 90 minutes the score was still 0-0. Sadly, in extra time, Stockton scored the only goal of the match and went on to the final, losing a week later to Long Itchington.

In mid April Stockton again played Whitnash, this time in the final of the Garland Invitation Cup, played at Moreton Morrell on Easter Monday, in front of a large crowd. Stockton scored an early goal and then a second, but Whitnash scored from a penalty before half-time. In the second half, it was reported that Horley in the Whitnash goal was "magnificent" and made several excellent saves but the score remained the same. So for the second time in a few weeks, Stockton had beaten Whitnash and the team and village-supporters had been disappointed.

Despite the fact that only the Stockton team was awarded medals, the Leamington Spa

Courier reported that "both teams drank out of the cup, amidst much cheering for Mr Garland" so at least the Whitnash heroes had a little glory.

In other years the Whitnash football team did win local cups, but somehow those disappointed lads of 1908 'flew the flag' for Whitnash in a most determined manner which I (and perhaps teams of today?) find quite inspirational.

THE RUGBY CLUB

Many of the Rugby Clubs in the area were re-formed in the early 1960s and this included Whitnash. In 1962 Old Warwickians Glen Hales and Michael Jacobs set up Whitnash RFC within the framework of the Sports and Social Club ——— Michael was already chairman and secretary of the football section and Glen had been cricket section treasurer for several years.

In 1962 the new team played a few matches at the end of the season, their first match being against Lockheed on Sunday April 15th. The match was played at the Tachbrook Road Ground and later a local paper carried a report on the match which began,

THIS PHOTOGRAPH OF THE FIRST XV WAS TAKEN ON 29TH NOVEMBER 1963 AT WHIT-NASH. Left to right, the back row is Michael Jacobs, Norman Todd, Doug Coulton, Ron Edden, Paul Brant, Peter Brant, Geoff Morris, Hilton Elgie and Fred Ogilvie. The front row is Stan Clark, Mark Robottom, Pete Enstone, Glen Hales (Capt), Jim Spence, Mick Penman and Tony Fine. Unfortunately the team lost 11-3 to Leamington A. that day! (MJ)

48

"Congratulations to Whitnash, the newly formed village team, who beat Lockheed II 8-3 in the first game."

Mike Jacobs was skipper and he led from the front scoring a try himself and converting another try scored by David Schofield.

The club became affiliated to the RFU and Warwickshire Union during the 1962/3 season and by 1964 was regularly fielding two sides and attracting new players. However, in 1967, a disagreement forced the club to look for a new ground and eventually this was found at Harbury where Mike Jacobs was then living. The club then became known as Whitnash and Harbury RFC but after a while the reference to Whitnash was dropped.

Glen Hales and John Bromley did much to ensure the club's survival at this stage and in later years it went from strength to strength. Players from Whitnash were still attracted to the club and recently John Hughes, the present Secretary of the Whitnash Sports and Social club, described how he had played for the club (although not the first team) some years ago. The Rugby Club is still going today ———-although sadly it has nothing to do with Whitnash.

IN MAY 1993 THE TEAM FROM WHITNASH COMBINED SCHOOL WON THE MID-WARWICKSHIRE SCHOOLS FOOTBALL LEAGUE. From left to right, the back row is Mark Mulroney, Mark Smith, Christopher Brown, Danny Thomas, Gurinder Mann, Dean O'Reilly, Darminder Rainu and Amandip Dhadda. The front row is Christopher Bradley, Garry Levis, Lea Connolly (Capt) Matthew Leahy and Richard Butcher. Absent from the photograph was Simon Griffin. (Photograph courtesy of Leamington Spa Courier)

WORLD FAMOUS LONG DISTANCE RUNNER, CAVIN WOODWARD WAS HONOURED IN HIS HOME TOWN WHEN WOODWARD CLOSE WAS NAMED AFTER HIM. Having taken up athletics in 1963, thirty years later Cavin was running his 200th Marathon/Ultra event. In the 1970s he won many world class races and broke several world track records, in particular the world track record for 100 miles in 1975 in a time of 11 hours, 38 minutes 54 seconds. His enthusiasm and love of his sport must surely give inspiration for the young people of Whitnash. (Photograph courtesy of Leamington Spa Courier)

THE CAVIN WOODWARD TROPHY WAS PRESENTED TO THE YOUNG SPORTS PERSONALITY OF THE YEAR IN WHITNASH AND IN JANUARY 1994 IT WENT TO 11 YEARS OLD JAMES COX. Mayor Bernard Kirton is seen presenting James (right) with the elaborate trophy and Darren Neal, also 11 years old, had a certificate as Runner-Up. James is the grandson of local historian, the late Gerald Cox and amongst other things, he is a most accomplished centre forward in football and athlete, particularly the 800 metres. In 1994 James helped St Margaret's C.E. Middle School to win the school league before he transferred to Myton School. Darren is also an accomplished footballer and athlete. (Photograph courtesy of the Leamington Spa Courier)

102 YEARS IN PHOTOGRAPHS 1893 -1995

In this section the history of over a century is summarised in pictures of people, buildings and activities. No text is necessary and the pictures and captions tell all.

ALTHOUGH I CANNOT POSITIVELY IDENTIFY ANYONE ON THIS PHOTOGRAPH OF WHITNASH SCHOOL IN 1893, THE BUILDING IS EASILY RECOGNISABLE. I find the whole group fascinating, especially the four boys in the front row with their hob-nailed boots. (GC)

THIS PHOTOGRAPH OF THE BARRACKS (TAKEN AROUND 1905?) ALSO SHOWS MANY OF THE PROUD INHABITANTS. "Holly Cottage" is on the right and this whole row was situated to the right of the playground of old Whitnash School. The Barracks were demolished around 1939, most of the former inhabitants having already been re-housed in new houses in Hall's Close.

(Reproduced by permission of Warwickshire Museum)

THE PLOUGH AND HARROW INN HAS NOT CHANGED MUCH BUT EVERYTHING ELSE HAS!
Since this photograph was taken in the early years of the 20th century Cotterill's Cottage to the
right of the inn and the bottle store to the left have both been demolished and the huge tree
overshadowing everything else was removed in the 1930s when the Heathcote Road houses were
built. (Reproduced by permission of Warwickshire County Council, Department of Libraries and
Heritage, Leamington Library and Bert Usher)

THIS FAMILY GROUP OF THE MASTERS FAMILY WAS TAKEN OUTSIDE HOME FARM IN
1910. With several generations represented it forms a delightful group. (MM)

THIS GROUP OF CHILDREN WITH THEIR DECORATED PRAMS, TRICYCLES AND WHEEL-BARROWS WERE STANDING ON THE CORNER OF THE VILLAGE GREEN CLOSE TO WHERE ST MARGARET'S HOUSE STANDS TODAY. The date would appear to be 1923 for one of the placards reads "God Bless the Prince of Wales" and that was the year he visited the Leamington and Warwick District. The brick building at the top left was the former blacksmith's forge —— only demolished in 1989. (GC)

REG MARRIOTT AND ONE OF BILL MASTERS' PIGS POSE IN GREEN FARM IN THE 1930s! Until the 1950s pig sties like these shown here were a common sight on farms and children delighted in climbing up to peer at the pigs inside. (MM)

*"I USED TO PINCH SWEDES. FROM IN THERE TO NIBBLE ON MY WAY TO SCHOOL"
CONFESSED AN ELDERLY RESIDENT RECENTLY! She was referring to the barn on the left
which was often used to store root crops. This photograph, taken in the 1920s when the population
of Whitnash was only 580, seems to capture the tranquillity of daily life in a typical Warwickshire
village. Although the barn has long since been demolished, Watts Cottages to the right and Green
Farm beyond still remain.(MM)*

*THIS HAPPY SNAP TAKEN IN THE 1930s SHOWS A GROUP OF WHITNASH CHILDREN
STANDING OPPOSITE TO OLD WHITNASH SCHOOL AFTER THE MAYPOLE CEREMONIES.
The boy in the blazer with the flags is Bill George and the boy on the right is Albert Parker. The May
Queen is Cicely Summers, the King in his splendid hat is Ron Foster whilst to Ron's left is Sheila
George, Tony Tabor and two unknown children.(WG)*

*THIS PHOTOGRAPH SHOWS MR PALMER'S STABLE, TWO HOUSES AND A BARN BELONG-
ING TO HOME FARM AROUND 1939. It was taken by Phyllis Turner of Leamington who says she
borrowed a camera from a Daily Mirror photographer. These buildings stood to the right of Glamis
Cottage in Whitnash Road on a site now occupied by maisonettes. (PT)*

*THE REAR OF HOME FARM LOOKS ALMOST IDYLLIC IN THIS 1930s PHOTOGRAPH! Today,
although the main house remains, most of these outbuildings are gone and Palmer Road now occu-
pies the field where the cattle once grazed. (MM)*

THE RATHER DILAPIDATED THATCHED ROOF BELONGED TO THE BARN OF HOME FARM. This photograph was taken in 1939 by Gordon Evans from the opposite direction to that depicted at the top of page 55.(GE)

*THESE COTTAGES NEAR GREEN FARM ARE NOW JOINED AND KNOWN AS
"LUPIN COTTAGE" ON ACCOUNT OF THE NUMEROUS FLOWERS WHICH
STILL GROW IN THE FRONT GARDEN. This snap was taken in 1939 by Gordon
Evans who once lived in Avon Road and now lives in Southam.(GE)*

58

THE WHITNASH NATIONAL FIRE SERVICE UNIT WHICH OPERATED DURING THE SECOND WORLD WAR IS SHOWN HERE IN A YARD NEAR TO THE BUNGALOW NUMBER 21 IN THE HEATHCOTE ROAD. *From right to left the back row is Mr Underhill (Snr), Mr Hill, Mr Underhill (Jnr), F. Roberts, W. Roberts, J. Dolden, G. Marlow, D. Jacobs, and A. Martin. The Front Row is S. Thornton, A. Bachelor, R. Hall, J. Bullock, P. Smith, and S. Addicott. S.Thornton was a well known threshing- machine proprieter and Percy Smith became a prominent local councillor after whom Greville Smith Avenue was named. (MJ)*

THIS FASCINATING SNAP OF RURAL LIFE WAS TAKEN IN THE LATE 1940s ON A SITE NOW OCCU-PIED BY PART OF THE CAR PARK IN FRONT OF THE HOME FARM CRESCENT SHOPS. The four happy members of the George family are from left to right Jennifer George, Sheila Waters (née George) Lilian George and Tony, Sheila's son. Hay ricks, like the one to the right, were once a very common sight in Whitnash. (WG)

THIS PAINTING COMPLETED BY C.E.PARKIN IN 1941 SEEMS TO CAPTURE MUCH OF THE HAPHAZARD CHARM OF ENGLISH RURAL ARCHITECTURE. The rear view of half-timbered, seventeenth century Green Farm, presents an interesting contrast with the older stone tower of the church beyond. (Reproduced by permission of Warwickshire County Record Office)

THIS PHOTOGRAPH SHOWS THE COMMITTEE AND SOME OF THE GUESTS AT A NEW YEAR PARTY FOR THE DARBY AND JOAN CLUB IN 1955. *From the left I believe the back row to be Mrs Jacobs, Mrs Percox, Mrs Bedford,, Mrs Marlow, ? , ? , Mrs Seekings Mrs Eden, ?. The front row is Sam Watts, Mrs D.H. Brown, Mrs Hall, ?, Harry Cox whilst the two people in the foreground are unknown. (MJ)*

ANOTHER DARBY AND JOAN GROUP PARTY IN THE WOMEN'S INSTITUTE HUT IN THE 1950s SHOWS MR CHERRY(LEFT) OF CHAPEL YARD WITH MRS CHERRY BESIDE HIM. *The names of the other guests I do not know for sure.(PH)*

THIS GLORIOUS SHOT OF HOME FARM WITH THE OLD BARN ON THE RIGHT AND THE OTHER OUTBUILDINGS TO THE LEFT, WAS TAKEN BY THE LATE BILL ARMSTONG AROUND 1959. Home Farm and its barn were still intact, but the wooden fence in the foreground meant that "The Homestead" was already being tiled and renovated to form "Elderfield". (JW)

"I CRIED WHEN THEY DEMOLISHED THAT BEAUTIFUL COTTAGE" —— SO SAID ONE WHITNASH RESIDENT TO ME RECENTLY. This charming photograph, taken by the late Bill Armstrong, shows " Cotterill's Cottage" in a most picturesque setting in the late 1950s. The cottage stood to the right of "The Plough and Harrow" and it was demolished in the 1960s. (JW)

THIS SNAPSHOT PROBABLY TAKEN IN THE 1940s SHOWS THE TWO SEVENTEENTH CENTURY, HALF TIMBERED COTTAGES FROM A DIFFERENT ANGLE. Said to have been "accidentally demolished by a reversing JCB" it makes me very sad to think that the picturesque cottage on the right was destroyed for no good reason. Even today the site is still empty! (GC)

THIS YPA SOCIAL TOOK PLACE IN ST MARGARET'S HALL IN THE MID 1950s. *From left to right the back row is Margaret Gleave, Ian Chard, Sheila Gray, Joey Bond, Aileen Gray, Michael Gleave, Mr Marsh, Ian Maycock, Margaret Jones, Paul Yarwood, Rev. Gleave (Rector), Derek Bedford, Eve Smith, Michael Cockburn, Stella Trindall, Rodney Layhe, Ann Trindall, Michael Jacobs and Valerie Taylor. The middle row is Carol Critchley, Judy Williams, Shirley Jones, Janet Bubb, Hazel Hart, Barbara Pearson and Ruth Morby. The front row on the floor is Ken Kitchen, Tony Syvret, Billy Scott, Tony Fine, Peter Fretwell, Glen Hales and David Hewins. (ML)*

WHITNASH BRANCH LIBRARY IN FRANKLIN ROAD OPENED ON 22ND MARCH 1962. *Shown here at the official opening (apparently some weeks later as the weather appears to be warm) are members of Whitnash Parish Council and Mrs Elizabeth Hulme, Chairman of the W.R.D.C. From left to right are Mr C. Mullard, Mr P. Smith, Mrs E. Hulme, Mrs J. Armstrong (now Warmington), Mrs J. Pritchard, Mrs P. Fisher, Mr H.W. Box, and Mr L. Burrows. (JW)*

MANY OLDER RESIDENTS OF WHITNASH WILL RECOGNISE FAMILIAR FACES ON THIS PHOTOGRAPH OF A VISIT BY THE W.I. TO THE WEDGWOOD FACTORY AROUND 1960. From the left the front row is Mrs Cox, ?, Mrs Tobias, Mrs Moore, Miss Dagleish, ?, Mrs Groom and Mrs Pearson. Mrs Russell is at the left of the second row with Jackie Warmington (then Armstrong), Mrs Tew, Mrs Carter on the right, with Mrs Hall behind them. Mrs Dolden and Mrs Jacobs are on the left of the back row and Mrs Murray is behind Mrs Carter but I am afraid I am unable to name the rest. (JW)

DURING THE 1960s THE THREAT OF A NUCLEAR ATTACK WAS TAKEN VERY SERIOUSLY AND THIS PHOTOGRAPH SHOWS AN EXERCISE CARRIED OUT BY WHITNASH TOWNSWOMEN'S GUILD FOR FEEDING PEOPLE IN THE EVENT OF JUST SUCH AN ATTACK. From left to right the group is Josie Foy, Betty Stephens,? , Joyce Wyatt, Isabelle Loveitt, Jackie Warmington (then Armstrong), ?, Beryl Dunn, Eileen Pailing, Margaret Felgate, ?, ?, and Joan Wykes. (JW)

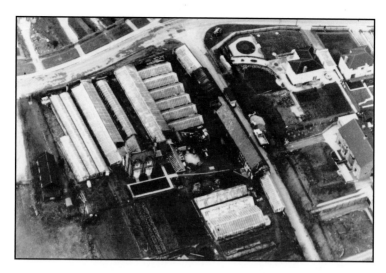

FOR MOST OF THE 20TH CENTURY, THERE WAS A NURSERY AT THE TOP OF GOLF LANE AND FROM THE 1920s ONWARDS, THESE PREMISES WERE RENTED BY THE SEEKINGS FAMILY. In the 19th century the land was occupied by a farm and farmbuildings, some of which were incorporated into the nursery. This aerial photograph, taken in the early 1960s shows the extensive greenhouses as well as the family house and garden which once occupied the land now covered by houses in 'The Seekings'. (DS)

EVERYONE SEEMS TO FALL IN LOVE WITH THIS WINTER VIEW OF THE TRADITIONAL VILLAGE GREEN NEAR ST MARGARET'S CHURCH. This photograph was taken by the late Bill Armstrong in the 1960s. (JW)

IN JULY 1985 BERYL SPERRING GAVE UP THE LEADERSHIP OF THE ST MARGARET'S
MOTHER AND BABY GROUP WHICH SHE HAD BEGUN SOME 9 YEARS EARLIER. At this
farewell party, Beryl can be seen centre front and slightly left, behind her is Jill Barker of Avon Road
who kindly lent me this photograph. (Photograph courtesy of Leamington Spa Courier)

IN APRIL 1983 THERE WAS A GATHERING IN "THE PLOUGH AND HARROW" WHEN A TANKARD PRESENTED TO TIM LYCETT SOME YEARS EARLIER WAS RETURNED TEM-PORARILY TO WHITNASH. Tim had emigrated, the tankard being presented as a leaving present. However within a few years Tim's wife and son died and when Tim himself died, the tankard was returned to England to Tim's niece. The back row is from left to right P.C. Brian Dobson, Paul Hanson, Derek Seekings, Gerald Cox and Walter Hassan. The front row is the landlord of "The Plough", Eveline Gunn, Les Burrows, Tim's sister and Tim's niece. (Photograph courtesy of the Leamington Evening Telegraph)

ON APRIL 25TH 1990 THE DARBY AND JOAN CLUB HELD THEIR 40TH BIRTHDAY PARTY IN WHITNASH COMMUNITY CENTRE. Mrs Elizabeth Bronckaerts, the Service Head of the Warwick Branch of the Women's Royal Voluntary Service which organised the party, can be seen in the dark suit cutting the cake and Phyllis Hodgkins, the local organiser, is standing on the extreme left. Amongst the members can be seen many Whitnash stalwarts including Mrs Yarwood and Frances Gibbs. (Photograph courtesy of Leamington Spa Courier)

IN MARCH 1993 THE WHITNASH POLICE OFFICE IN FRANKLIN ROAD WAS OFFICIALLY OPENED. From left to right are Councillor Bernard Kirton (Mayor), P.C. Tony Gooch, Superintendent Richard Lyttle, and Special Constable Nigel Palmer. Harry Hughes (currently Mayor) was Whitnash "Bobby" from 1948 to 1966 and later Brian Dobson served for 15 years. Tony Gooch filled the post from 1990 to 1995, and he still serves on the Governing body of a local school. Locally born Mandy Saysell is the current holder of the post and recently "Special" Nigel Palmer completed 8 years of service. (Photograph courtesy of Leamington Spa Courier)

ON 30TH APRIL 1993 A SPECIAL EVENING SERVICE WAS HELD IN ST MARGARET'S CHURCH TO MARK REV. TONY GARDNER'S 25TH ANNIVERSARY AS RECTOR OF WHITNASH. In this photograph taken some days earlier, Canon Gardner is displaying a special needlework picture, presented to him by the Mothers' Union and designed by Edna Figgitt one of the members. (Photograph courtesy of Leamington Spa Courier)

TRADITIONALLY THE MARRIAGE OF THE RECTOR'S DAUGHTER WAS A GREAT EVENT IN WHITNASH AND SO IT WAS IN AUGUST 1993 WHEN RACHEL GARDNER MARRIED. Having lost her sight some years earlier, Rachel was attended throughout the ceremony by her guide dog Dulcie, a black labrador retriever cross in addition to bridesmaid Heather Bowley. Rachel's parents Rev. Tony Gardner and Irene Gardner are shown on the right of this most delightful wedding photograph and Rachel's husband Robert Clifton is shown left. (Photograph courtesy of Leamington Evening Telegraph)

IN MARCH 1994 JAMES ALLEN AGED 15 OF THE 1ST WHITNASH TROOP WAS PRESENTED WITH THE CHIEF SCOUT'S AWARD. District Commissioner Don Sullivan is pictured left with David Bramston, Assistant Scout Leader on the right. James had been a keen scout for 8 years and had to perform a number of tasks, including some community service, to win the award. He is still very keen on scouting and is now an Assistant Cub Scout Leader at Bishop's Tachbrook. (Photograph courtesy of Observer Newspapers)

IN DECEMBER 1994 THESE BEAVER SCOUTS TOOK THEIR PLEDGE TO "BE HONEST AND KIND" AT A CEREMONY ORGANISED BY WHITNASH SCOUT LEADER JO-ANN BRAMSTON. The troop is attached to Whitnash Methodist Church. From the left, the back row is Christopher Clark, James Protheroe, Thomas Nicholls, Steven Kavanagh; the second row is Andrew Watson, James Hart, Oliver Adams Matthew Cunliffe; the third row is Richard Calcutt, William Pound, Timothy Robbins, Ben Langley; the front row is Christopher Nicholls, Andrew Reading, Simon Beckett and Richard Ingram. (Photograph courtesy of Observer Newspapers)

74

TWO INFLUENTIAL CHARACTERS AT THE ST MARGARET'S DAY CELEBRATIONS IN 1994.
JACKIE WARMINGTON (LEFT) WAS CHAIRMAN OF THE WHITNASH SOCIETY AND REV.
CHARMAINE HOST, IS ASSOCIATE MINISTER OF ST MARGARET'S CHURCH. Born in Surrey
and coming to Whitnash in 1951, Jackie was previously married to Bill Armstrong who died in 1979.
A talented individual, Jackie, who was a local J.P. for 21 years and a Whitnash Parish Councillor
for 6 years, once completed "a hole in one" at the Golf Course in Whitnash! Charmaine came to
Whitnash in 1994 and was one of the first of the women deacons to be ordained Priest at Coventry
Cathedral in April 1994. She has a husband Ian and two teenage daughters. (Photograph courtesy
of Leamington Spa Courier)

*THERE WAS A MOST APPRECIATIVE CROWD TO WATCH THE MORRIS DANCING BY
'CHINEWRDE' IN FRONT OF WHITNASH CHURCH ON ST MARGARET'S DAY JULY 20TH
1994. Here piano-accordion player Andrew Sharpe of "Chinewrde" is surrounded by Eileen
Roberts (front left) and Barbara Turnock (front right) with Mabel Race, Norma Bourne, Beryl
Griffin, Janet Ticehurst and others in the background. (Photograph courtesy of Observer
Newspapers)*

76

THERE WAS AN EXCELLENT TURN OUT FOR THE PARADE THROUGH WHITNASH TO COMMEMORATE THE 50TH ANNIVERSARY OF VJ DAY IN AUGUST 1995. SOME OF THE MARCHERS CAME FROM ELSEWHERE AS THERE WERE NO OFFICIAL COMMEMORATIONS IN LEAMINGTON OR WARWICK. An open-air service outside St Joseph's R.C. Church was followed by a parade to the War Memorial led by a piper and the Mayor of Whitnash. (Photograph courtesy of Leamington Evening Telegraph)

AT THE WAR MEMORIAL THE MAYOR OF WHITNASH, COUNCILLOR HARRY HUGHES, LAID A WREATH. (Photograph courtesy of Leamington Spa Courier)

78

AUGUST 1995 WAS THE 25TH ANNUAL CARNIVAL IN WHITNASH
AND FIVE YEAR OLD CASEY CRUTCHLEY IS PICTURED HERE
WITH TWO TALL FRIENDS FROM THE WHITNASH TWINNING
ASSOCIATION'S MARDI GRAS FLOAT. *Carnival Queen, Susan Duane,
led the line-up in a horse and trap and the Mayors of Whitnash, Warwick,
Southam and Leamington, followed by fifteen floats, formed a colourful
procession. Thousands of people turned up on the Acre Close Playing
Field to enjoy the stalls and mini-funfair. (Photograph courtesy of
Observer Newspapers)*

SNIPPETS

I thought it would be interesting to include a selection of miscellaneous items and one of the most fascinating of these is a late case of the old punishment of lewbelling (lewd bellowing?) strangely reminiscent of a Thomas Hardy novel. Often the punishment involved making an effigy of the man and /or woman judged to have loose morals, but the Whitnash villagers simply made a great commotion.

Around the end of the First World War a man and a woman were "escorted" to the parish boundary past old Whitnash School late one night by a group of villagers. They were angry that a hardworking woman who kept a sweet shop in Chapel Yard and her daughter had been wronged by a female lodger and the daughter's husband when he came back from the war. The villagers banged pots and pans to cause a great commotion as they were determined to force the guilty woman out.

Mrs Hilda Avis now aged 94 remembers taking part. *"We went to the house and banged on the door and forced her out. Then I ran with them ——-we ran her out of the village."*

****

During the 1930s there was a tramp named Tommy Sargeant, who was periodically to be seen sitting on the steps of the old Methodist Chapel by Chapel Green, playing his tin whistle. At that time the Fosse Way was still a gated road and Tommy used to earn himself some money by opening the gates.

There are various people who recall Tommy, including Derrick Seekings and Gordon Evans.

****

In St Joseph's Roman Catholic Church in Whitnash is a memorial window to the martyr St Oliver Plunkett and his story is a most interesting, albeit sad one. Born in Ireland and educated in Rome, he was appointed Bishop of Armagh in 1669 and soon became respected by both Catholics and Protestants in Northern Ireland. In 1678 he was arrested and falsely charged with high treason and after being found guilty in 1681, he was hanged, drawn and quartered at Tyburn in July 1681. His body is now at Downside Abbey in Somerset, whilst his head is now in the Oliver Plunkett Memorial Church in Drogheda, Ireland.

****

On Sunday March 31st 1963 a Quarter Peal of 1260 Plain Bob Doubles was rung at St Margaret's Church as a farewell to the Curate and his wife, Rev. and Mrs R.B. Hems. The team was Jim Harris, Linda Taylor, Ian Stevens, Percy Oram, Ian Maycock, and Ian Box.

On 12th January 1964 a Quarter Peal of 1260 changes was rung for Sunday Mattins and the completion of 54 years of Sunday School teaching by Mrs Robbins who had then retired.

****

IAN BOX, A LIFELONG RESIDENT OF WHITNASH, HAS GIVEN SEVERAL TALKS TO THE WHITNASH SOCIETY OF WHICH HE IS HONORARY SECRETARY. Ian gave his first talk on the history of Whitnash to St Margaret's YPA in 1963 whilst he was still a teenager! (Photograph courtesy of Observer Newspapers)

:**

s poem is one of a number written by talented Thomas Roberts, the present organist and choirmaster at St Margaret's.This recent poem was inspired by a talk on the legends and history of Whitnash given to the Whitnash Society in early 1996 by Ian Box.

Whitnash

Whitnash of the Doomsday,
t'was on a ley line set;
Home of the wise men,
whose Parliament once there met;
Of ash woods, and the withy,
for both of these had been;
Joseph Arch and the meeting,
by the smithy, on Church Green.

From St Peter's Mount,
and east by 'Royal Way'
Mill dam field, by the brook,
Still there for us today;
Monks of old bought a bell,
to bless, beside the stream;
T'is said it fell into a well,
be this legend, or the dream!

Thomas J.W. Roberts
20th February 1996

****

Finally I would like to include just a selection of memories related to me by Whitnash residents and ex-residents.

"In 1924 all the schoolchildren went to the Wembley Exhibition in London on the train. Each child was given some money but some spent it on Bournville chocolate or two Kensitas Cigarettes for 1d."
Octogenarian Fred Meades (now resident in Coventry) in a telephone conversation to me in 1993.

****

"Bert's father bought Glamis Cottage in 1918 and the cottage had a huge chimn Bert and his father used to have to sweep it by going up it themselves, dressed* a *clothes, hats and masks. There was a trapdoor inside the Inglenook...*
Bert's mother used to put a jug on her kitchen window sill. Tad Palmer (wh v-*shed was adjacent to the cottage) used to fill it up with warm, fresh milk straigh* iis *cows."*
Mrs Bayliss of St Catherine's Crescent in 1993, speaking of her husband Be family

****

"My parents told me that they had the first taxi wedding in Whitnash. My fathe. Reginald was a member of St Margaret's Church Choir until the late 1920s and before the First World War he was a keen member of the village football team."
Doris Alcock aged 77 of Landor House in 1996.

****

"I wonder how many people will remember or indeed ever be aware that in the early 1930s the Royal Air Force sent an aeroplane on a possible "recruiting drive" and that this landed in Mr Master's Field to the south of Leamington Cemetry. I was at Leamington College at the time, as were his sons, and we were given the morning off from school to witness a flying display with a talk at school in the evening."
Mr L.W. Grimwood of Summerton Road in 1993.
(In the 1950s and 1960s he was Sec. of Whitnash Cricket club and his late wife Noreen was the First District Commissioner of the Guides and Brownies for the Whitnash District in 1968.)

****

"When I was a child we used to recite this rhyme 'Willy Willy Woodbine/ Bring me good luck/ Please put a sixpence/ Under my foot' as we tapped an empty Woodbine packet with our feet when we found one on the ground... I used to call the area where St Catherine's Crescent is now "Black Ash" because there was a black ash path there."
Marjorie Webb of St Catherine's Crescent in 1993

****

"So much happened in the W.I. Hut particularly during the second World War ......two whist drives a week were held there and endless parties and fundraising. ...I used to cycle to Whitnash over the L.M.S Railway line, through Waverley Road, Northway and "The claps" which had a cornfield on the right and brook and allotments on the left. ... I remember Rev. Gleave and his sale of goat's milk for children with infantile eczema ...To keep the children healthy and active we used to spend whole days in fields in Whitnash and we gathered mushrooms and blackberries and watercress in the brook".

Mrs G.M. Langley aged 85 of South Leamington in 1994

****

"On V.E. night in 1945 'Tad' Palmer drove along the Heathcote Road standing up in his cart. Everyone cheered as he drove past and a boy who was sitting on the back axle fell off. The horse then bolted and didn't stop till it reached the Heathcote Lane".

'Mick' Marlow (once of Heathcote Road, now resident in Kenilworth) in 1993.

****

"The surge of interest in the Whitnash bells in the 1950s was due, in the first place to Michael Gleave, the Rector's son. After a term at Cambridge where he himself had learned to ring he came home and valiantly set about teaching some of the young people in the village. Until then, the bells had only been chimed...

Old Mr Hauley had learned to ring many years before and was therefore delighted to practise his skill once again ...he spent a lot of time pricking out changes on paper in order to help the new band of aspiring ringers, by now in the capable hands of Percy Oram.

There followed a year or two in a blaze of local publicity; this was because the majority of the young ringers were girls and, in those days, female bell ringers seemed quite an oddity. The band became quite used to visits from photographers and then seeing their exploits recorded under such headlines as "Belles in the Belfry...

Whitnash has a first class set of bells in a very attractive ringing chamber and let us hope that the tradition of ringing so ably revived by Michael Gleave and Percy Oram, will continue to flourish."

This was written in 1994 by Jean Pailing (née Addicott) who is now resident in Kent. Just for the record, old Mr Hauley died in July 1963 at the age of nearly 98. As he rang regularly even when in his nineties, at the time he was said to be possibly the oldest bell-ringer in the world.

****

"You can have your age but we prefer our time when we were able to go violeting and gathering cowslips and primroses.

You knew everyone! When you got on the bus, everyone spoke to you. There was a lot of joy in the old village."

Olive Dingley of Landor Road, now aged 87, was recalling life in Whitnash in the 1930s and 1940s.

THE FORMATION OF THE WHITNASH SOCIETY

In July 1993, just a few weeks after the launch of "Beneath the Great Elms" a group of enthusiasts decided to form a civic society in Whitnash. Following one or two preliminary meetings, the first meeting proper was held in "The New Hall" of the Whitnash Sports and Social Club, on Monday July 5th 1993, when around 40 enthusiastic people asked many questions.

A Committee was elected and although there have been a few changes, on the whole the committee has remained basically the same for the three years of the Society's existence.

The aim of the Society was to enhance the built up parts of the town and protect the best of the rural features which remain.

Shortly after its formation, the Society became a member of the Civic Trust and membership has increased steadily.

The first Secretary who has had the onorous task of writing numerous letters is Ian Box and during late 1993 and early 1994 various complaints had to be made to official bodies. Whitnash residents had noticed that the name "Whitnash" had been omitted from telephone directory addresses and there were problems with other directories and official maps. Eventually, after numerous letters, the Whitnash Society established that the problems had arisen after a mistake concerning Post Codes and when this was rectified, the Whitnash Society felt that its first major battle had been won on behalf of residents of the Independent town.

FOR AROUND 10 YEARS JOHN CHIPPERFIELD PROUDLY CARRIED ON THE TRADITION OF PRINTING IN WHITNASH WHICH WAS BEGUN BY CANON YOUNG IN VICTORIAN TIMES. John is seen here with the printing press installed in the old school room (now St Margaret's Church Centre) on which numerous items including parish magazines were printed by him, each month, in his spare time. Sadly John died in January 1996 but his advice on the printing of books was invaluable to me in the preparation of this volume. (TR)

The first Chairman of the Society was printer John Chipperfield and he conducted the first meetings with his usual brand of humour. Within a year, however, although he remained a member of the committee, John had to stand down because of ill health and sadly he died very suddenly in January 1996 aged 62. He was a talented performer at the Whitnash Society's Christmas entertainments and his beautiful tenor voice was heard in the church choir and in the local choir known as Cajjatie from the initial letters of the names of the original members.

In 1994 the enthusiastic Jackie Warmington took over as Chairman and when she decided to stand down because of ill health, her energetic husband Stan agreed to help out and take on the difficult task. Eileen Roberts has been Treasurer since the beginning and Ann Moffat has been the Minutes Secretary. Other Committee members since 1993 have been Nell Davies of Greenhill Road, Gerald Cox (deceased 1994), Jill Barker of Avon Road and myself. In 1994 Derek Seekings joined the committee and in 1995 he was joined by Paul Yarwood and Daisy Mills.

FINAL THOUGHTS

In 1991 the official population of Whitnash was given as 7,297, but since then it has increased considerably. At the present time, hundreds of new houses are planned for Whitnash —- —some close to the site of the Water Mill near the brook, others along the Warwick Border at Heathcote near the famous Boundary Oak and others on the site of former allotments near Heathcote Road. It has been suggested that the large number of new houses will swamp the spirit of individuality amongst the residents of Whitnash.

However, I believe that this will not be the case for as the population increases, so does the influence of the residents and I can sense there is a new optimism abroad. I have not had room to dwell on this in this book, but Whitnash residents have a long history of fighting for their rights. In 1898 the villagers argued long and hard about problems with the churchyard and 97 years later Whitnash was featured on Midlands T.V. News at least twice during 1995 because residents, The Town Council and the Whitnash Society spoke out against unsympathetic proposals for the town.

It is my experience that almost without exception, people are proud to say that they belong to Whitnash and many ex- residents are keen to revisit the place where they were happy. It is my hope that this book will help residents and visitors alike to understand a little more of the fascinating history so that in the future residents can appreciate such sites as those of the holy well, water mill and the hill fort.

I think the last word should go to a resident who once remarked "I do like living in Whitnash —— it is a civilised place to live." Somehow that thought just about sums up what I have been trying to say in this book!

(opposite page)

IN 1995 THE WHITNASH SOCIETY COMMISSIONED TALENTED KIM WOOD, A 19 YEAR OLD ART STUDENT FROM LANDOR ROAD, TO COMPLETE A SERIES OF LINE DRAWINGS WHICH COULD BE USED ON NOTELETS AND TEA TOWELS.

WHITNASH

St. Margaret's Church

St. Margaret's
Old School House

Lupin Cottage

The Plough and Harrow

Home Farm

Glamis Cottage

Green Farm

Watts Cottage

ACKNOWLEDGEMENTS

'The Whitnash Society' has been extremely helpful concerning the publication of this book. Various members have lent photogaphs or shared reminiscences with me and I am especially grateful to all the members of the Committee.

It is impossible for me to name all the individuals who have given assistance with this book but I would like to give special thanks to ─────── The Rector, Freda Cox, Hilda Avis, Betty and Les Adams, Bill George, Frances Gibbs, Gordon Evans, Marjorie and Reg Marriott in Oxford, Ted and Ethel Masters in Worcestershire, Nancy Bailey, Ann Box, Phyllis Hodgkins, Michael and Valerie Jacobs in Dorset and Jean Pailing in Kent. Also Whitnash Town Council, the first Mayor, Bernard Kirton, and his successor, Michael Morris, have been very supportive, as has the present mayor, Harry Hughes.

The County Archivist and all the staff of the Warwickshire County Record Office where I conducted much of the research have been particularly helpful, especially Jerry Weber, the Chief Conservator who copied many of the photographs which are reproduced here. I would also like to thank Gary Archer, the Local Amenities Officer at Leamington Library and Lesley Kirkwood, the Local History Librarian at Warwick Library.

It was sheer good fortune which alerted me to the existence of a photograph album in the Record Office at Hawarden containing various photographs of life in Whitnash in Canon Young's time. I would like to thank Mrs Josie Hughes of Whitnash, Miss Elizabeth Pettit of Flintshire Record Office and especially Ms Judy Corbett of Llanrwst, Denbighshire for allowing me to reproduce items from this album. A few months ago the album, along with numerous other items in the Galltfaenan collection was moved to the Denbighshire Record Office in Ruthin where it is to be kept in future.

Miss J. Greenwood has kindly undertaken the role of proof reader and I am greatly indebted to her and other friends, including Miss M. Lang, who have given invaluable help and advice.

SOURCES OF PHOTOGRAPHS FROM PRIVATE COLLECTIONS

IB Mr I.Box, GC the late Mr G. Cox, GE Mr G. Evans, WG Mr W. George, FG Mrs F. Gibbs, MJ Mr M. Jacobs, ML the late Mrs M. Lomas, MM Mrs M. Marriott, IM Mr I. Maycock, TR Mr T. Roberts, DS Mr D. Seekings, PT Miss P. Turner, JW Mrs J. Warmington, MW Miss M. Webb, AV Mrs A.Vick

BIBLIOGRAPHY

Victoria County History of Warwickshire Volume 6
The Antiquities of Warwickshire
> by Sir W. Dugdale 1656

Pagan Celtic Britain
> by Anne Ross (Constable, London 1992)

The Old Straight Track
> by Alfred Watkins (First Published 1925)

The West Midlands in the Early Middle Ages
> by Margaret Gelling (Leicester University Press 1992)

Trees and Woodland in the British Landscape
> by Oliver Rackham (J.M. Dent 1976)

A History of Warwickshire
> by Terry Slater (Phillimore 1981)

The Oxford Dictionary of Saints
> by David Farmer (Oxford 1978)

The Place Names of Warwickshire
> by Gover, Mawer, and Stenton (Cambridge 1970)

A History and Description of the Parish of Whitnash
> by Rev. J.R. Young (Whitnash Press 1865)

Twenty Years of Recitations (Whitnash Press 1871)
Historic Warwickshire
> by J. T. Burgess (1875)

Rural Romance, Quaint Tales of Old Warwickshire
> by T.B.D. Horniblow (The Courier Press 1923)

How Old is Your House?
> by Pamela Cunnington (Alphabooks 1980)

A Pictorial Record of Great Western Engines Vol. 1
> by J.H. Russell (Oxford 1975)

Various editions of the Warwick Advertiser, Leamington Spa Courier, Leamington Spa Observer and other newspapers.

APPENDIX

THE ORIGIN OF SOME WHITNASH ROAD NAMES

1) Named After Old Whitnash Families (Some of the families once owned the land
    on which the houses were built)

Allibone Close	Markham Drive
Ashford Road (and Gardens)	Murcott Road
Cotterills Close	Osborne Court
Franklin Road	Palmer Road
Halls Close	The Seekings
Landor Road	Summerton Road
Masters Road	

2) Named After Specific People with a Whitnash Connection
    (d. after name indicates person is deceased)

Anderson Drive (Lt Jean Anderson, U.S Airforce d. 1945)
Armstrong Close (W. Armstrong, voluntary worker d. 1979)
Box Close (H. W. Box. local councillor d. 1991)
Brunel Close (I.K. Brunel, GWR Chief Engineer, d. 1859)
Burrows Close (H. L. Burrows, local councillor d.)
Canon Young Road (Canon Young, Rector 1846 -1884)
Clarkson Drive (J. Clarkson, Brownie Leader)
Crutchley Way (K. Crutchley, local councillor)
Dawson Close (A. Dawson, local councillor d.)
Dobson Lane (B. Dobson, former local policeman)
Evans Grove (E. A. Evans, local councillor)
Gleave Road (Rev. C.H. Gleave, Rector 1935 -1967 d.)
Greenhill Road (Rev. N. Greenhill, Rector 1609 -1650)
Greville Smith Avenue (P.G. Smith, local councillor d.)
Holmes Road (J. Holmes, local councillor)
Kirton Close (B. Kirton, local councillor)
Morse Road (Rev T. Morse, Rector 1732 -1784)
Morris Drive (M.J. Morris, local councillor)
Mullard Drive (C. Mullard, local councillor d.)
Woodward Close (Cavin Woodward, famous athlete)

3) Roads Retaining Former Field Names
    Rowley Road —— Rowley Field (rough arable or grassland)
    Moorhill Road — Moorhill Field (barren waste land)
    Whitmore Road ·—— Whitmore Field (land with a white surface)

N.B. THESE LISTS CONTAIN ONLY A SELECTION OF ROAD NAMES.
MANY OF THE PEOPLE REFERRED TO ARE MENTIONED IN THIS BOOK
OR "BENEATH THE GREAT ELMS".

WHITNASH TOWN COUNCIL
(as at 1st May 1996)

Mr H.A.R. Hughes ——— Mayor
Mrs E.A. Evans (Deputy Mayor)

Mr I.A.H. Box	Mr M.J. Morris
Mrs J.A. Falp	Mr N. Roberts
Mr R.N. Hawke	Mr J.R. Short
Mr J.A. Hughes	Mr B.A. Smart
Mr P.T. Jackson	Mr D.E. Stocks
Ms C.S. Kelly	Mr K.A.W. Williams
Mr B. Kirton	

Clerk to the Council ——— Mrs D.C. Dalby

****

DISTRICT COUNCILLORS

Mr P.T. Jackson, Mr B. Kirton, Mr J.R. Short

COUNTY COUNCILLOR

Bernard Kirton of Avon Road, the County Councillor for Whitnash for 15 years, was elected Chairman of Warwickshire County Council on May 14th 1996. This is the first time since the formation of the County Council in 1894 that the Councillor for Whitnash has been given this honour and the publishers of this book would like to offer Mr Kirton hearty congratulations.

BY THE SAME AUTHOR
A Tour of St Margaret's Church, Whitnash
Published 1992 (Obtainable from the Church)
She Dyed about Midnight (Warwick) 1992 Brewin Books
Beneath the Great Elms (Whitnash) 1993 Brewin Books
Kings of Warwick 1995 Brewin Books
Acorns, Oaks and Squirrels 1996
Warwick Preparatory School

90

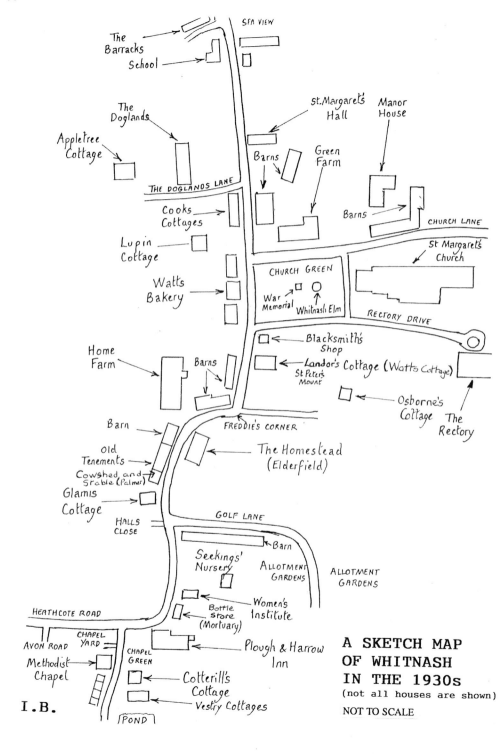

The Barracks
School
SEA VIEW
The Doglands
Appletree Cottage
THE DOGLANDS LANE
St. Margaret's Hall
Manor House
Barns
Green Farm
Barns
CHURCH LANE
Cooks Cottages
Lupin Cottage
Watts Bakery
CHURCH GREEN
War Memorial
Whitnash Elm
St Margaret's Church
RECTORY DRIVE
Home Farm
Barns
Blacksmith's Shop
Landor's Cottage (Watts Cottage)
St Peter's Mount
Osborne's Cottage
The Rectory
Barn
FREDDIE'S CORNER
Old Tenements
Cowshed and Stable (Palmer)
Glamis Cottage
HALLS CLOSE
The Homestead (Elderfield)
GOLF LANE
Barn
Seekings' Nursery
ALLOTMENT GARDENS
ALLOTMENT GARDENS
Women's Institute
HEATHCOTE ROAD
Bottle Store (Mortuary)
AVON ROAD
CHAPEL YARD
CHAPEL GREEN
Methodist Chapel
Plough & Harrow Inn
Cotterill's Cottage
Vestry Cottages
POND

I.B.

A SKETCH MAP
OF WHITNASH
IN THE 1930s
(not all houses are shown)

NOT TO SCALE